A Christian Contract With AMERICA

For The Soul of Our Nation

A Christian
A Contract With
AMERICA

For The Soul of Our Nation

Tim Lee

Liberty
HOUSE
PUBLISHERS

P.O. Box 10307 • Lynchburg, VA 24506

A CHRISTIAN CONTRACT WITH AMERICA
For the Soul of our Nation

Cover and Book Design: Lee Fredrickson

Library of Congress Cataloging-in Publication Data

Tim Lee
A Christian Contract With America / by Tim Lee
p. cm.
1. America 2. Politics 3. Title

ISBN 1-888684-01-1

Printed in the United States of America

Acknowledgment

American history was made by decisions; decisions of faith, decisions of courage, decisions of direction from great men who knew the decisions they made often meant the chance of death. Such was the decision of fifty-six men when they signed their names to a document in Philadelphia, July 4, 1776. They knew by doing so, it would bring freedom to all Americans, or have each of them hanging from British gallows. By making that decision, one nation, under God, came into existence.

Alliances of other great men and women have fought, and even now fight, to keep America, one nation under God: The Moral Majority, the Eagle Forum, Christian Coalition For America, Focus on the Family, Concerned Women for America, and still many, many more. I thank God for their decisions of courage and faith to stand apart for the soul of our nation. I thank God for the spirit in the heart of every soldier who has fought, or will fight for the cause of freedom and of our great nation. I thank God for the courage He gave me personally, when I lost both legs to the cause of freedom.

When the British crown appointed their own governor, Governor Gage, he sent a personal messenger to call on Samuel Adams. His directive was to stop Adams' opposition to the Crown. Adams could cease his opposition and receive great benefits from personal bribes, or continue to risk certain death. Samuel Adams reply was a decision of courage when he wrote: "Then you may tell Governor Gage that I trust I have long since made my peace with the King of Kings. No personal consideration shall induce me to abandon the righteous cause of my country; and tell Governor Gage it is the advise of Samuel Adams to him, no longer to insult the feelings of an exasperated people."

I thank God for my personal desire to see America brought back to one nation under God, and for the decisions, the courage and vision of all those who have helped me with the writing, as well as the production of this book.

I pray that God would continue to provide the courage to decision making men and women, to stand with me for God and Country!...for is there not a cause?   —Dr. Tim Lee

Table of Contents

Introduction

The sudden and dramatic success of the Republican Party's *Contract with America* has gained instant recognition. Forged by conservatives within the party, the *Contract* called for immediate changes in the "politics-as-usual" style of congressional affairs in Washington, D.C.

Thank God for the foresight of those who developed this *Contract,* and thank God for those 367 candidates who signed it. Their courage is formidable, their determination admirable and their insight commendable. Despite all the obstacles they have already overcome, there is a limited political agenda. We need to go much further!

The Christian Coalition has proposed a ten-point *Contract with the American Family.* It, too, is powerful, insightful and commendable. It calls for respect for religious equality and an end to religious hostility. It also calls for the respect of family values, human life and public safety, but we need to go much further.

After meeting with hundreds of pastors from every corner of the nation, I am convinced that the Christian community needs to establish *A Christian Contract with America.* We need to commit ourselves afresh to defend and promote those Christian beliefs and values that are at the very heart and soul of the American public.

I am not calling for a *Contract* that excludes other religious beliefs that are part of our democratic republic. I truly believe in the freedom of religion for all people, but I believe it is high time that Bible-believing Christians step to the forefront of the spiritual awakening that America so desperately needs.

This book is a call to *action*! Many of us have wept and prayed. Now it is time to do something that can make a difference for our children and grandchildren. It is time for this generation to bless its succeeding generations. It is the midnight hour, and it is time to heed the midnight call!

Won't you join me along with thousands of others who have already pledged to honor this dramatic call to action?

—Dr. Tim Lee, Dallas Texas

Forward

Is There Still Hope For America?

by Jerry Falwell

I began to become very concerned about America's future two decades ago, not that I did not see the trends already in motion, from the outlawing of prayer in the schools back in 1962 and the tragic Supreme Court decision for legalized abortion (the killing of unborn human beings) in the *Roe v. Wade* case in 1973.

But in 1975 and 76 I took to the road with "I Love America" rallies, urging the Christian citizenry and everyone who loved this nation and who appreciated its heritage to rise up to preserve our values and traditions.

Now for these two decades I have continued to call for spiritual revival and to challenge Americans to vote for candidates who would not only pledge to continue our religious and traditional heritage, but would prove their sincerity after being elected.

In the late 1970s I formed *Moral Majority* and was strongly criticized in some circles for daring to "mix politics with religion." Many critics wrongly quoted the phrase "wall of separation between the church and state," as though it were constitutional law. It is not.

Presidents have taken the oath of office with their hands on the Bible since George Washington. The Ten Commandments adorn the walls of the Supreme Court building.

Our nation was founded by such as the pioneering Pilgrims and Christians of many denominations fleeing from religious persecution and desiring to worship God according to their consciences, and those who wanted freedom from oppression and a new opportunity. All of this has been well documented and is factual, although most of today's liberal schoolbook authors have sought to erase from our memories the truth of our religious foundations.

George Orwell's classic prophetic novel, *1984*, described a future government propaganda agency, which would remove paragraphs from history, erase people from photographs, and rewrite history to suit the national party line and the new culture. This was called NEWSPEAK.

Many of us supposed this was mere speculative fiction, but now the "Orwellian Newspeakers" are writing American history textbooks. . .and much of what they write **is fiction.**

As I have crusaded for America's values and traditions, while still always preaching the unvarnished Gospel of Christ, over the last 20 years, many others have emerged as spokesmen for our mutual causes. Some were active as conservative Christians with political interests prior to my maximum involvement, but most have burst on the scene since 1980.

In spite of all the negative signs and in spite of the continuing deterioration of our moral fibre, I believe there is still hope for America.

There is still the possibility of a great spiritual awakening in this country with God divinely intervening for revival. On the Liberty University campus during the 1994-95 year, revival broke out. On scores of college campuses and in hundreds of churches, nonstop prayer meetings among the young people and others have taken place, seemingly in a spontaneous manner. I pray for real revival and call for fasting and prayer in the spirit of II Chronicles 7:14 every day.

Likewise, we must not retreat into the closet of prayer and just stay uninvolved.

We must be the "salt of the earth" and the "light of the world."

We must take action to preserve our heritage, our religious freedom (under vicious attack by the ACLU and other anti-Christian movements, which would decimate our Judeo-Christian ethic and our traditional biblical morality), and our very nation from being overrun by immorality, evil, crime and sin.

I am very excited about Evangelist Tim Lee's marvelous new book *A Christian Contract With America.*

This spiritual, godly dedicated American war hero and

veteran of the Vietnam conflict, has pinpointed the very ills, and the national scandals that threaten our future.

In this book he deals with abortion, pornography, drugs, crime, homosexuality, lack of medical ethics, media perversion, and the loss of a will to defend our liberties.

So impressed was I when reading Tim Lee's manuscript that in my heart I decided to launch *Liberty House Publishers* and make this dynamic evangelist's work our very first project.

Read this book carefully. Underline important ideas!

Then be resolved to be involved!

Christians must not give up their civil rights, their freedom of speech, their freedom of religion, their freedom to vote according to their consciences, their freedom to peaceably assemble and to petition their government for a redress of grievances.

Christians must not falsely assume that since the Bible predicts apostasy, moral declension, drug addiction, violence, theft and increasing immorality in "the last days," they can just accept the inevitable and let our country slide down to the outskirts of hell.

No! A thousand times, no!

There is hope!

Hope for revival! Pray for it!

Hope for a better America!

Let us pray and work, vote and speak, crusade and inform, encourage and support causes and candidates, which can restore America to her moral and spiritual moorings.

This book can better equip you to fight the good fight of faith.

"Now it is high time to awake from our sleep, for now is our salvation nearer than when we believed."

Awake and get into action "for God and country."

Jerry Falwell, Chancellor
Liberty University
Lynchburg, Virginia

Yes, I will be glad to sign the "Christian Contract With America." Where is the dotted line?

—Dr. D. James Kennedy
Senior Minister
Coral Ridge Presbyterian Church

Chapter 1

Why A Christian Contract?

God has blessed us with a great spiritual heritage. Pilgrims, Puritans, pastors, revivalists and evangelists have heralded the message of God's grace across the heartlands of America. From "sea to shining sea," churches have sprung up all over this nation to declare the glory of God and the blessing of God's people. Every element of our economy and our society has been blessed as a result.

But America is at a great crossroads today. She sits on the very precipice of potential ruin. Crime is rampant in our streets. Our young people are caught in the snare of drugs and immorality. Our families are torn apart by the worst divorce rate in human history. We can no longer sit back and be silent! We must speak up now before it is too late! The time for action has come, and we must respond now!

Spiritual priorities of our nation

The time has come for the Christian public to insist that we restore the spiritual priorities of our nation. Recently, 367 Republican candidates signed their names on the dotted line to call America to restore its bonds of trust between the people and

13

their elected officials. Their dramatic *Contract with America* called for an end to political evasion and posturing. It presented a powerful agenda for national renewal, and it came in the form of a written commitment with no fine print.[1]

The liberal media attempted to decry this *Contract with America* as empty rhetoric...campaign slogans...and political jargon. They could not have been further from the truth. The Contract spoke right to the heart of the major political problems in our nation. It was written in plain language, and it detailed specific promises.

On September 27, 1994, the *Contract with America* was publicly unveiled when over 300 Republican candidates for the U.S. House of Representatives stood on the west front of the U.S. Capitol and publicly pledged to bring a political rebirth to the American Congress. Those candidates came from all over America to sign their names to a blueprint for action based upon five principles that defined their basic philosophy of American civilization...[2]

- individual liberty
- economic opportunity
- limited government
- personal responsibility
- national security

Using those principles as a basis of operations, House Republicans outlined a vision for America's future. That vision seeks to renew the "American Dream" by redefining the role of government in American life. Those principles called upon the candidates to work together to communicate a vision of clearly defined themes, programs and legislative initiatives aimed at earning them the honor of becoming the majority party in 1995.

At a time when public confidence in Congress was at an all-time low, the Republican hopefuls dared to call America back to sanity, honesty and decency. In place of typical political rhetoric, they offered a detailed agenda for national renewal.

Quoting Abraham Lincoln, the first Republican president, the signers of the contract pledged to act "with firmness in the right, as God gives us courage to see the right."[3] They committed themselves to make us all proud of our American political system and the values which it espouses.

Change for a better America

In order to enact their agenda for change, the Republicans proposed ten bills for a better America. They also promised to enact these bills within their first one hundred days in office. They included:

Fiscal Responsibility Act

A balanced budget and tax limitation amendment and a legislative line-item veto to restore fiscal responsibility to the Congress.

Taking Back Our Streets Act

An anticrime package including stronger sentences, effective death penalty provisions, and provisions for additional law enforcement to keep people secure in their neighborhoods.

Personal Responsibility Act

This legislation was designed to discourage illegitimacy and teen pregnancy by prohibiting welfare to minor mothers, and enacting a two-years-and-out provision with work requirements to promote individual responsibility.

Family Reinforcement Acts

Stronger enforcement of child support, tax incentives for adoption, strengthening the rights of parents, stronger child pornography laws, and tax credits for elderly dependent family care.

American Dream Restoration Act

A $500 per child tax credit, repeal of the marriage tax penalty, and middle class family tax relief.

National Security Restoration Act

Restoration of essential funding to strengthen our national defence and maintenance of our international credibility, as well as a "No U.S. troops under UN command" provision.

Senior Citizens Fairness Act

Repeal 1993 tax increases on Social Security benefits, raise the Social Security earnings limit which forces senior citizens out of the workplace, and includes the provision of private long-term care insurance.

Job Creation and Wage Enhancement Act

Small business incentives, capital gains cuts, neutral cost recovery, strengthening of the Regulatory Flexibility Act and reforms to create jobs and raise wages.

Common Sense Legal Reforms Act

Reasonable limits on punitive damages, reform of product liability laws, "loser pays penalties" to restrict the endless cascade of litigation.

Citizen Legislative Act

Term limits to replace career politicians with citizen legislators, thereby really giving the vote to the people themselves.

It was a bold and courageous incentive by the Republican candidates. They put their political careers on the line by standing up to the administration's tax-and-spend assault on American families. It was a call to end 40 years of Democratic control of the Congress.

Election Day, November 8, 1994, marked a dramatic turning point in American history. Voters sent a powerful and undeniable message to Washington, D.C. No more politics as usual! Their mandate for change resulted in the Speaker of the House being defeated for reelection for the first time in 130 years! Not only were liberal Democrats overwhelmingly defeated, but not one single incumbent Republican was defeated. The vote was a mandate for a new agenda, a new America, a new hope for the future. But for all of its incredible impact, the Contract with America is basically limited to our nation's social, economic and political needs.

The need for a spiritual awakening

America also needs a spiritual awakening that will shake her self-sufficient pride, bring her to her knees, and transform her citizens' hearts and lives. *Los Angeles Times* columnist, Cal Thomas, has said: "The way to transform a nation is not by politics alone."[4] We must demonstrate the power of true Christianity to a society gone mad on the emptiness of secularism, atheism, socialism and liberalism.

I believe the time has come for Christians to stand up, speak up, and demand to be heard. More than ever before, we must have real heroes; men and women who will stand for what is right, and who will stand against what is wrong, no matter what the cost. Like our Founding Fathers, we must be willing to say: "We pledge our lives, our fortunes, and our sacred honor."

I gave my two legs to defend this nation's honor and her personal commitments, and I would do it again!

I'm a flag-waving American! There has never been another country like America in the entire history of the free world, but America today is spiritually sick. Like Israel of old, it may be said: "The crown is fallen from our head: woe unto us, that we have sinned" (Lamentations 5:16).

Our national flag, birthed in the blood of the Revolution, has been the symbol of our freedom. It has flown victorious over the frozen fields of Valley Forge, the bloodstained farms of Gettysburg, the muddy trenches of Europe and the steamy jungles of Southeast Asia. It has endured attack, assault and ridicule. It was meant for waving; waving in triumph!

God pity the nation that forgets the blood and suffering its own people have endured to keep it free. God have mercy on those who despise the very freedom which allows them to speak against this nation. But I tell you, they are not the problem. The real problem in America today is that professing Christendom will not stand up and demand better. It has long been observed that all that has to happen for a nation to fall is for good men to do nothing!

This book is a call to do something! It is...
- a call to national revival
- a call to repentance
- a call to faith.
- a call to commitment, and, above all, it is
- a call to spiritual change

17

King Hezekiah came to the throne of Israel after a time of spiritual decline. 2 Chronicles 29 describes the quick and powerful transformation that he brought. The Scripture records:

> "And he did that which was right in the sight of the Lord" (v.2). He immediately opened the doors of the house of the Lord (v. 3). Then, he gathered all the preachers (Priests and Levites) and called upon them to make a new covenant (contract) with God (v. 10). He demanded that they cleanse the House of God. He called for national revival (v. 18).

Next, Hezekiah called upon the politicians (rulers) and demanded national repentance and reconciliation (v. 20). First, he challenged the preachers to get right with God. Then, he challenged the politicians to get right with God. By the time he finished his sweeping reform, the Scripture says: "And Hezekiah rejoiced, and all the people, that God had prepared the people for the thing was done suddenly" (v. 36).

That is exactly what we need today: a sudden and dramatic national repentance and revival, one that literally transforms the soul of our nation, one that glorifies God, and brings His blessing on us.

A spiritual contract with America

As politics go, the Republican's contract is impressive indeed. It raises the hopes and dreams of all conservative Americans, but it is still only a collection of proposed legislative bills that are collectively labeled a "contract." In fact, three bills from the Contract have already been passed. But as good as it may be, it does not go far enough to cure the moral and spiritual ills of the American public. The contract we need is a Spiritual Contract.

Improved politics and line-item vetoes will not save America. We are still a nation of what George Grant calls, "declining schools, decaying cities and diminished expectations."[5] Our moral conscience is dead, our national behavior is morally bankrupt, and crime is rampant in our cities. We are bombarded with daily reports of murder, rape, robbery and violence.

The secular *Index of Leading Cultural Indicators* observes:

The condition of our culture is not good. Over the last three decades we have experienced substantial social regression. Today the forces of social decomposition are challenging - and in some instances overtaking - the forces of social composition, and when decomposition takes hold, it exacts an enormous human cost.[6]

Several years ago Robert Hutchins observed the trends of the times and wrote:

Relativism, scientism, skepticism, and anti-intellectualism, the four horsemen of the philosophical apocalypse, have produced that chaos in education which will end in the disintegration of the West.[7]

We have continued on that course for the past twenty-five years, and we are now dangerously close to the kind of spiritual and moral collapse from which we shall never recover. We must act now in order to turn our nation around before it is too late. Theologian Francis Schaeffer observed:

America is now a nation in which Christianity is thought to be just one more item on the consumerist menu of special interest offerings that may help some individuals prosper and succeed in the never-ending American pasttime: The quest for self-realization without limits and without feelings of guilt or responsibility for the ultimate consequences of one's actions.[8]

The prospects for the future are frightening! The spectrum of moral disintegration, the collapse of the traditional family, the spread of AIDS and other viral diseases; the increase of criminal violence, terrorist attacks and even the possibility of the resurgence of communism are enough to make one's soul sick.

The answer does not lie in politics alone. George Grant is right when he says:

Politics is important, but it is not all-important. Most ordinary people know that only too well. They always have. They always will.[9]

Let me go even further and add that Christians, of all people, ought to know that with great certainty! We cannot hope to cure America's ills without God. Only He can change her heart, regenerate her soul, and redirect her national life. Nothing short of a national revival can turn America around. Only a spiritual awakening of the deepest sort can prevent us from rushing headlong over the precipice of national destruction.

We must be the ones who call America back to God
We must act now! We cannot wait for politicians to help us. They can only deal with political and judicial matters. Thank God for those politicians who are standing up for what is right. But the vast majority of politicians are not going to bed at night weeping over our national sins, and our great moral decay.

We must be the ones who call America back to God, back to righteousness, and back to moral sanity. We need a renewed commitment to the spiritual mandate to recapture this nation from the very forces of Hell itself.

I agree with the appeal Jerry Falwell makes when he says:

> More than ever before in the history of humanity, we must have as heroes those men and women who will stand for that which is right and stand against what is wrong, no matter what it costs.[10]

In this *Christian Contract with America*, we are calling for sudden and dramatic change. Just as the Republican candidates did in their contract, so I believe we must do the same. Just as they addressed ten key issues, so I believe we are facing ten key issues in the spiritual battle for the soul of America:

1. Abortion
We must stop the senseless murder of millions of unborn Americans. It is the height of hypocrisy when our leaders sit and weep over the tragic slaughter of innocent little children in the recent bombing of the Federal Building in Oklahoma City. Those same leaders, including our own President, condone the

20

ongoing carnage of abortion that kills over one million equally innocent unborn babies every year in this nation.

2. Pornography

We must work to prohibit the distribution of pornography which demeans our women, perverts our youth, and destroys our families. This multibillion-dollar industry is largely responsible for the degradation of the heart and soul of our country.

Liberal politicians, educators and religionists have condoned, supported and promoted this filthy enterprise that shakes its naked fist in the very face of God.

3. Drugs

The drug crisis is at an all-time high in America. The so-called "War on Drugs" has been a total failure! It is time we declared real war on drugs with severe jail sentences, and death penalties for major distributors. We must quit playing around with this poison before it kills the next generation of Americans.

4. Crime

The streets of America's major cities are no longer safe for her citizens. Murder, rape, robbery and violent crimes are at an all-time high. This is no time for more rhetoric. Criminals only understand one language. We need to expand the powers of law enforcement, pass stronger laws against potential criminals and reenact the death penalty as the ultimate deterrent to crime.

5. Homosexuality

Homosexuality is the symptom of a spiritually sick society. It is a rebellion against the very character and nature of God. Flaunting this perverted life-style before impressionable children is the ultimate form of child abuse. It is detrimental to every tenant of the Christian home and society. We must love the sinner, yet condemn his sin as a perversion of God's created order.

6. Family Values

America is only as strong as her families. When the family falls, society will collapse. We must do everything we can to encourage the national acceptance of strong family values. We must minister to the hurts and struggles of single and divorced Americans, yet we must also hold high the banner of the family. These are the values and principles that have made America great. Also, we must pledge ourselves to do all we can to defeat political and social leaders who stand against our family values.

7. Lack of Medical Ethics

America faces a crisis in the area of Bioethics, which must be reversed. Many are now calling for assisted suicides and euthanasia (so-called mercy killings - the elimination of the elderly and the infirm). Others are advocating fetal tissue transplants from aborted babies. Still others are calling for genetic experimentations without proper consideration of its ethical implications. All too often this is being done in the name of medical progress, yet we must insist that it not be done at the expense of human life.

8. Media Perversion

The immoral impact of America's television, movies and media are a national disgrace. Many of the Third World nations are horrified at our tolerance of such perversion. We have disgraced ourselves, our morals, our bodies, and have done this over the airwaves of our own nation. Morally concerned Americans must insist that we clean up TV, movies, magazines, etc.

9. National Defense

There can be no doubt that Ronald Reagan's greatest legacy will be the buildup of our national defenses which led to the fall of Communism. We have already made foolish cutbacks, assuming the Cold War to be over. Our greatest protection for the future is a strong national defense. We must also continue to do everything necessary to promote peace through strength.

10. National Revival

At the core of all our nation's greatest needs is the need for revival. We must stop playing church "as usual." Our nation's internal problems are the direct result of her spiritual problems. God's people must humble themselves, pray, seek His face and turn from their wicked ways. Only then can we have a future!

"Government cannot make us good. All that government can do is restrain evil. Since there is no law that can make you love me, there must be laws to keep you from killing me. God's ideal is a free church in a free state. The government must do what it alone can do so the church is free to do what it alone can do."

—Dr. Adrian Rogers
Bellevue Baptist Church
Cordova, Tennessee

Chapter 2

Abortion
The Silent Holocaust

Abortion is wrong! The broken bodies and scattered limbs of dead babies lying in dumpsters behind abortion clinics is wrong. The assault of the suction machine ripping the baby from the womb is wrong. The slashing tentacles of the curette slicing the unborn child to pieces is wrong. Killing babies for profit is wrong. Aborting the unborn for one's own personal convenience is wrong. Let there be no question where the Christian community must stand on this issue. Abortion is wrong and it must be stopped!

On January 22, 1973, a bloody stain appeared on the soul of our nation. On that day, the Supreme Court legalized abortion on demand in the case of *Roe v. Wade*. On that terrible day, the highest court in our land legalized abortion, and, as Tom Elliff has observed, "On that day America...sold its soul to the devil."[1]

The Declaration of Independence states that all men are created with certain inalienable rights, including the fundamental right to life, yet that basic right was torn from the heart of the American people by one of the most terrible decisions ever rendered by the Supreme Court of the United States. It was as

25

though they had taken a knife and cut that basic right to life out of our nation's founding document. From that point onward, the ethical landscape of America turned blood-red.

Changes to America

Subsequently several changes occurred that have not been reversed since that terrible day - January 11, 1973.

1. Abortion on demand became the law.

The dreadful reach of the abortionist's hand has been aided by the government of the United States. Not only is abortion lawful, but many forms of protest against abortion are now unlawful. Over 5,000 babies are killed every day in America's hospitals and abortion clinics.

2. Our tax dollars now subsidize abortions.

National and state tax revenues are used to support massive welfare abortions, and we who are fundamentally opposed to abortion are helpless to prevent our tax dollars from supporting it. Think of it! The taxes from your hard-earned income are going to support murder! Even though you may be opposed to the federal funding of abortion, you are helping pay for it every single day.

3. Parental consent for minors is now eliminated.

Minors who cannot receive any medical assistance at school - not even an aspirin - without parental consent may request an abortion without their parents' knowledge. School counselors are instructed to refer pregnant teens to Planned Parenthood and they, in turn, are free to recommend an abortion without parental consent.

4. Late term abortions are permissible.

Abortions can be performed as late as the final trimester of pregnancy. In other words, children who are old enough to live outside the womb may now be legally killed in the womb.

In one of the most hypocritical ethical perversions imaginable, the medical community will fight to save the life of a seven-month-old prematurely born infant, while taking the life of a seven-month-old "fetus."

5. **Abortion is now the contraceptive choice of millions of women.**

Ninety percent of all abortions are blamed on "unwanted pregnancy." Forty percent of all abortions are repeat abortions for pregnant mothers. Many women are now using abortion as a convenient method of birth control.

Tom Elliff points to the parallel to the terrible practice of child sacrifice conducted by pagan nations[2] - a practice which God clearly condemned. Israel's ancient Canaanite neighbors threw their children into the fiery arms of gods like Molech who demanded child sacrifice as an act of worship.

Today, parents are sacrificing their unborn children on the altars of secularism, humanism and hedonism. Nearly 30 million babies have been slaughtered in the past twenty-some years since abortion was legalized in America.

The supreme injustice

God's Word has not changed! His moral laws have not been repealed. "Thou shalt not kill" is still on the law books of heaven. It still resounds from the court of Divine Justice, and it stands emblazoned on the eternal statutes of the Kingdom of God. It is God's "Contract with America" and all other nations that claim to know Him.

Human life is precious to God. He created it, Jesus Christ died to redeem it, and the Holy Spirit acts to preserve it. Anyone who violates the fundamental right to life has violated the very nature and character of God.

The Bible instructs us: "Deliver them that are drawn unto death, and those that are ready to be slain" (Proverbs 24:11). We have a responsibility to prevent the taking of innocent human life. If we who name the name of Jesus Christ do not speak up on their behalf, who will? My heart is broken every time I think of the 56,555 brave men who lost their lives in Vietnam, but my heart is broken even more when I realize that the same number of innocent children are killed by abortionists every two weeks in America.

We cannot turn a deaf ear to their silent cries. We dare not pretend it is not so. The scripture warns: "If thou sayest, Behold, we knew it not; doth not he that pondereth the heart consider it? And he that keepeth thy soul, doth not he know it? And shall not he render to every man according to his works?" (Proverbs 24:12). God knows, and God is keeping the records, and He will not let America go unpunished for her indifference.

Liberals talk about choice—until it comes to the choice of those who disagree with them. Then, they deny us our choice under the misguided rhetoric of "censorship." Yet, God tells us what choice to make in Deuteronomy 30:19, when He says: "I call heaven and earth to record this day against you, that I have set before you life and death, blessing and cursing: Therefore, choose life, that both thou and thy seed may live."

While the word abortion does not appear in the Bible, the scriptures speak very clearly about the significance of the unborn. When Mary, pregnant with the unborn Savior, visited her cousin Elisabeth, pregnant with the unborn John the Baptist, the Bible says "the babe leaped in her womb; and Elisabeth was filled with the Holy Ghost" (Luke 1:41). The unborn children were real people. John the Baptist rejoiced in the Savior's presence, though they were both still in the womb. In fact, the Bible says of Jesus that He would be filled with the Holy Ghost even from his mother's womb" (Luke 15).

The argument is always raised by pro-abortionists that the pregnant woman has the right to choose what to do with her body. But the Bible reminds us that no true believer, male or female, has the right to do whatever he or she wants to with their bodies. 1 Corinthians 6:19-20, says: "What? Know ye not that your body is the temple of the Holy Ghost which is in you, which ye have of God, and ye are not your own. For ye are bought with a price: therefore glorify God in your body, and in your spirit, which are God's."

We do not have a right to do whatever we want with our bodies. We have been created by the life-giving power of God, and we have the capacity to pass on that gift of life, but we dare not think it is ours to give or take. It is His decision, not ours. There is no such thing as being "Pro-Choice." The very term is a misnomer. Those who choose to abort their children are taking the choice away from them forever. They are willfully choosing death and destruction. They are taking every opportunity of life away from those precious children.

Abortion is wrong!

The Bible clearly condemns the "shedding of innocent blood" as wrong. Why then is there such an avid debate over this issue? Because some do not care if it is wrong. Their seared consciences compel them to shake their fists in the very face of God.

Others are ignorant of what abortion really involves. It is not just the removal of undesirable tissue from the body. It is the slaughter of innocent human life.

Our national conscience has been seared by guilt. Millions of Americans have a guilty conscience because they have participated in the atrocity of abortion. Millions more feel guilty because they have failed to speak up and defend the unborn. Our guilty silence has a deafening roar to it.

In many cases we have put the value of our own selfish pursuit of pleasure above the value of human life. "Let them die," they are really saying, "so I can have fun." What a tragedy! People are placing their own happiness above the happiness of others. They are throwing their babies out the window of life just so they can continue their irresponsible behavior.

I am convinced that if we allow the ruthless killing of preborns to spread, it will only be a matter of time until the elderly and the handicapped will go too. Let us value the priceless gift of life above the cheap chant of selfish "choice."

What really goes on in the abortion clinics is killing for convenience. Joseph Scheidler, founder of the Pro-Life Action League, has said: "Most of the women going into abortion clinics are not in any kind of danger; they simply want their own will and don't care about the consequences. They are getting rid of the evidence that they are living promiscuous lives."[3]

Mr. Scheidler has personally buried over 5,000 babies retrieved from abortion clinic trash dumpsters. Some of these babies were five, six and seven months old. Their bodies were ripped to pieces. Some were beheaded. All of them went through excruciating pain to satisfy some woman's desire not to be pregnant.

Objections answered

Abortion is the number one killer in the United States. More people have died because of abortion than died in all our nation's wars combined! It is the silent holocaust of our times, and it must be stopped.

But someone will always assert that there are difficult issues left unanswered concerning abortion.

Let's consider a few.

1. **No one knows when human life begins.**

Actually, we do know when human life begins - at conception. Prior to that, the male sperm has 23 chromosomes and the female egg has 23 chromosomes. But when they unite into 46 chromosomes, the result is a human being with a lifelong genetic code and identity of his or her own.

For the sake of argument, let's assume we don't know for sure when life begins. Common sense and human decency tell us to give the benefit of the doubt to human life.

For example, if you found someone lying along side the road and you weren't sure whether they were alive or dead, you wouldn't call the mortuary to take them to the funeral home. No, you would call 911, hoping there was a chance they might live.

2. **Doesn't the mother have the right to her own body?**

There is no moral right to commit murder. First of all, the baby is not part of her body, like her liver, lungs or larynx. The baby is an individual human being with its own separate body, identity and personality.

3. **Babies are not conscious personal beings.**

Yes, they are conscious before they are born. By six weeks after conception, the baby has its own brain wave. As early as three months the unborn baby can feel pain and pressure, and reacts to various stimuli.

4. **Better to abort a child than abuse one.**

There is no greater abuse than to murder a child! Stealing the life of the unborn is the worst form of child abuse. In the meantime, child abuse cases have increased while the number of abortions have gone up. Abortion shows such disrespect for life that it leads to worse abuse of the living.

5. We cannot legislate morality.

Every law on the books is the legislation of someone's morality. If the legislation of morality were inappropriate, then we should remove all laws against murder, crime, robbery, child abuse, incest and rape. These are laws that reflect moral beliefs and principles. Even laws that permit abortion are a result of someone's belief that abortion is a morally acceptable option.

6. Isn't abortion a religious issue?

No! It certainly involves one's religious beliefs, yet it is fundamentally a human issue. It involves the scientific issue of when does life begin. It also involves the ethical issue of how we ought to treat human life. It is not a Catholic, Protestant or Jewish issue. It is a question of who lives or dies!

7. Isn't it better for unwanted babies not to be born?

This question is based on the false assumption that all unwanted pregnancies will necessarily become unwanted babies. Even if the birth mother does not want to keep her child, there are loving families who would gladly adopt them. Dr. Norman Geisler has observed, "Just because we do not want someone to live doesn't mean we have the right to kill them."[4]

Consider this scenario

A teenage girl once became pregnant. She was engaged to another man who was not the father of the baby. Her family was poor, but had a fine reputation in her little community. How could she shame them? How could she put her husband-to-be through such humiliation? The quick solution would have been an abortion, yet the thought of an abortion never entered her mind. She decided to have her baby, endure the ridicule, marry her fiance, and ask him to raise her child. Her name was Mary. Her baby was Jesus!

The eyes of God

What God creates and fashions belongs to Him. He is the owner, creator and designer of His universe. In Psalm 139, King David of ancient Israel was overwhelmed with such thoughts - the greatness of God, the vastness of His universe, and the power of His Word. Then David personalized those lofty thoughts and compared God's creative majesty to the sanctity of a mother's womb.

"Thou hast covered me in my mother's womb" (v. 13), David declared. He referred to the covering of human flesh as God's protective provision for human life. In the secret domain of life's beginning at conception, David declares, "I am fearfully and wonderfully made." The psalmist of Israel surely considered man the unique creation of Almighty God.

Then David made an astonishing statement: "My substance was not hid from thee, when I was made in secret" (v. 15). The Hebrew word 'etsem, translated "substance," literally means "bones."[5] God saw the skeletal structure that would develop even before it was fully formed! This means the newly conceived individual is viewed in regard to his or her potential development - not as a mere speck of life.

Then, David went on to say, "Thine eyes did see my substance, yet being unperfect" (v. 16). This time the word rendered "substance" translates the Hebrew word golem, meaning "embryo."[6] It is a unique biblical term referring to embryonic human life. Think of it! God saw you when you were just an embryo-newly conceived human life. "Unperfect," meaning "undeveloped." God saw you at the earliest stages of human life, even before you began to grow and develop.

David goes even further. In verse 16, he writes: "in thy book all my members were written, which in continuance were fashioned, when as yet there were none of them." God has already recorded the genetic code of your body. He knows from conception the details of your human development - limb by limb and member by member. Every detail of your human body is recorded in heaven.

Whenever an abortionist takes his instrument of death and desecrates the womb of God's divine protection, he defiles the creation of God. His murderous hands remove the covering of

God's protection. They break through the divine canopy of protection for human life, and that murder is recorded in the annals of the books of divine judgment in heaven. Awaiting retribution on that day of judgment when "the dead, small and great, stand before God and the books were opened...and the dead were judged out of those things which were written in the books" (Revelation 20:12).

I shudder every time I read this passage! The omniscient eyes of God see into the womb of every pregnant woman in the world. He sees that embryo as human life, and in His divine knowledge, He sees it for what it will grow to be - a full grown person, and He sees all the potential of what that person will ever grow to become.

Then that also means that God sees that tiny person when the saline solution of the abortionist comes cascading like a flood into that womb and poisons that human being. It means that God sees the jagged edge of the abortionist's curette as it rips and pulls that helpless baby to bloody pieces - limb by limb. It means the ears of God hear his or her silent screams that cry out like Abel's innocent blood (cf. Genesis 4:10). Screams that reach the very courts of heaven itself!

It is every Christian's duty to cry out against this slaughter. This butchery. This terrible act of heathenism. This defilement of God's creation. It is time we said, "Enough is enough!" More Americans have died from the abortionist's knife than died in all our nation's wars combined (see chart). We cannot let their deaths go unchallenged. We must do everything legally possible to stop this carnage as soon as possible.

A Grim Reminder

Each cross mark represents 50,000 deaths
How does abortion stack up with all other American Wars?

Revolutionary War (23,324) .... +
Civil War (600,000) .... +++++++++++++
World War I (116,515) .... +++
World War II (545,108) .... ++++++++++++
Korean War (54,246) .... +
Vietnam War (56,555) .... +
ABORTION WAR (27,000,000) ....
+++
+++. +++++++++++++++++++++++
+++
+++
+++
++

33

Unimaginable cruelty

In 1979, a young woman took a nursing job in a Denver suburb of Colorado, for a doctor who specialized in obstetrics. She was soon shocked to learn of the number of abortions they performed on a regular basis. After a traumatic and broken-hearted experience, she was converted in a Denver church, and later shared this tragic story of her experiences:[7]

"The second week I was there, a 17 year old girl came in for her third abortion. She was using it for birth control. 'How come you don't use something else?' I asked. She said she didn't like other forms of birth control. She thought this was convenient and it was free because Medicaid paid for it...

We did several kinds (of abortions) there. We used suction up until 12-14 weeks. That (involved) a metal suction apparatus inserted into the uterus and poked around until the fetus was all sucked out. After about 12 weeks the fetus would be too big...We would dilate the cervix...then go in with tongs with an open spoon at one end. They would just grab parts of the baby and pull them off. The baby would bleed to death. They would get an arm or leg and the nurse would have to count everything that came out to make sure they got it all. It was horrible!

I remember one time we did a girl who was 12 weeks along, and as little as that baby was, you could see on the Sonogram, it was sucking its thumb. Twenty minutes later it was in a bottle of formaldehyde all sucked up. We showed the girl the picture and we all laughed.

In August 1979, right before I was converted, we got a lady who was 18 weeks along. We saved her until the very end of the day because she was so big. We knew she would bleed a lot and take a lot of time and effort to clean up. There was a big bucket at the end of the table to catch stuff. We had to take all the contents of that bucket, including the dismembered fetus and put it in formaldehyde.

The LPN ended up going in the bathroom and vomiting. I was standing there at the sink, crying my eyes out. 'My God,' I thought, 'we are all going to hell!' "

A few weeks later, Mrs. Griggs was converted to Christ in a church in Denver. She quit the doctor's office, and later she began to share her experiences with abortion. I know this is difficult to read, and difficult to think about. But what if you were that baby? Would you want someone to spare your life and give you a chance to live?

Diary of a fetus

I recently came across this anonymously written diary. It assumes the attitude of the newly conceived child:

October 5: Today my life began. My parents do not know it yet. I am as small as the pollen of a flower, but it is I already. I will be a girl. I will have blonde hair and blue eyes. Nearly everything is settled already, even that I shall love flowers.

October 19: I have grown a little, but I am still too small to do anything myself. My mother does almost everything for me, though she still does not know she is carrying me under her heart. But, is it true that I am not yet a real person? That only my mother exists? I am a real person, just as a small crumb of bread is still bread. My mother is, and I am.

October 23: My mouth is just now beginning to open. Just think - in a year or so I'll be laughing; and later I'll start to talk. My first word will be "Mama."

October 25: Today my heart began to beat. It will beat softly for the rest of my life; never stopped until I shall die.

November 2: I am growing continually. My arms and legs are taking shape but I must wait a long time before these tiny legs will raise me to my mother's arms; before these little arms will be able to embrace my mother.

November 12: Tiny fingers are beginning to form on my hands. How small they are! One day I will clasp my mother's hand, pull her hair, and touch her face.

November 20: Only today the doctor told my mother that I am living here under her heart. How happy she must be. You are happy, Mother?

November 25: My mother and father are probably thinking about a name for me; and they don't even know that I am a little girl, so they are probably called me "Andy." But I want to be called Barbara. I am growing so big.

December 10: My hair is growing. It is as bright and shiny as the sun. I wonder what kind of hair my mother has?

December 13: I am almost able to see, though it is night around me. When mother brings me into the world, it will be full of sunshine and overflowing with flowers. But more than anything I want to see my mother. How do you look, Mother?

December 24: I wonder if my mother hears the delicate beat of my heart? My heart is healthy. It beats so evenly: Tup-tup, tup-tup. You shall have a healthy daughter, Mother. I shall grow up to be a doctor and discover the cure for AIDS.

December 28: Today, my mother killed me!

What can we do?

We can win the fight against abortion without bloodshed, without violence, and without acts of hatred. Remember, many of these young mothers live right in your own neighborhood. She may be the girl who baby-sits your children, or checks your groceries at the corner store, or cashes your check at the bank. She may be a pastor's daughter or the mayor's niece.

She need not be an evil person. She has simply made a mistake. Oh, it is sin all right. But all of us have sinned, and God is still in the business of forgiving sinners. But one sin does not have to lead to another sin. That pregnant teenager or young woman has to make a decision that she will live with for the rest of her life.

When she finally has the courage to tell someone, she will almost inevitably be advised to get an abortion.

Right now a girl on your street, in your neighborhood, walking in a park, or sitting in a coffee shop may be crying out. Praying for someone to help her. Jerry Falwell tells the story of a girl named Gail in his book, *If I Should Die Before I Wake.*[8]

"Gail was standing on the wing of a 747 jetliner at a gate in Chicago's O'Hare Field when they found her. No one knows exactly how she got there. She was crying bitterly, and the police report read: "Her arms were reaching to heaven and her body was twisting and turning as if in terrible agony." Airport security personnel got Gail down from the wing and into a restraining area of the concourse. Gail later took a bus to the Liberty Godparent Home in Lynchburg, Virginia.

"I came to save my baby," she told Jim Shavely, the director. "I saw a movie on TV about what you do here, and I came to give it a try."

Gail was later converted to Christ just before she was due to deliver her baby. She had gone through four months of professional counseling, loving care in a local "shepherding" home, and personal study groups.

"I want to become a Christian before my baby is born," she told a friend. Several days later, her baby was born and placed for adoption with a loving Christian family.

Today, Gail is living a brand new life in a small town in Tennessee.

That story could be repeated thousands of times if enough churches would reach out compassionately to unwed mothers. We can and we must provide them with a better alternative. Then, ultimately we must vote our convictions. We must put people into office who will diligently work for a constitutional amendment to overturn *Roe v. Wade*. It can happen! It must happen for the children's sake!

Here are some positive steps of action we can take:

Pray. Intercede for innocent babies and the mothers and fathers who will decide whether or not to get an abortion. Pray for elected officials who will take the necessary legal action to prevent abortions on demand.

Write. Let your representatives in congress know how you feel about this issue. Don't underestimate the potential impact of calls and letters. The more calls and letters a congressman or congresswoman receives, the more they realize how important an issue is.

Distribute Literature. You can distribute pamphlets at clinics, hospitals, doctor's offices, schools, libraries, or door to door. Local pro-life groups can provide the necessary materials.

Picketing. Public demonstrations done in the spirit of love can bring the abortion issue to the attention of the public. It will also cause some to rethink their decision to abort. A "chain of life" demonstration can be very effective, but do it in love.

Talk to Your Doctor. Ask what stand he or she takes on abortion. Let them know your concerns. Support and encourage your doctor if he is opposed to abortions. If he favors them, you may want to consider changing doctors. Remember, people are not our enemies. It is the practice that is wrong.

Start a Crisis Pregnancy Center. If you have a local pro-life crisis pregnancy center, support it. Volunteer. Help out. Send money. If not, help get one started. A Christian-based crisis pregnancy center can offer free early pregnancy tests and personal counseling.

Vote Your Convictions. Register and vote! The decisions of national public policy are made by those who take time to vote. No vote - no power. No power - no influence. We must vote people into office who will vote for a constitutional amendment, and people who will vote pro-abortionists out of office.

We can't change society overnight. But we can change it one life at a time, one day at a time, one person at a time.

"History fails to record a single precedent in which nations subject to moral decay have not passed into political and economic decline. There has been either a spiritual awakening to overcome the moral lapse, or a progressive deterioration leading to ultimate national disaster."

—General Douglas MacArthur

Chapter 3

Pornography
Polluting the American Mind

Pornography is a $4 billion a year business in the United States alone. Much of the income from this money is used to influence legislators, the legal system, as well as the American public, in order to reduce the criminalization of pornography. Polls indicate that nearly 80% of all Americans oppose pornography. Yet, the porno plague is sweeping America!

Pornography is not a pleasant subject to discuss, but it is such a major problem in our nation that it must be discussed. The word, pornography, comes from the Greek words *porneo* (prostitute), and *graphen* (to write). Originally the term referred to the activities of those who traded in illicit sex.

Twenty five years ago the term meant writing, pictures, and other images used to excite sexual arousal. Now the dictionary brings an even broader meaning that includes deviations, perversions and abnormal behavior.

Pornography offers a dangerously distorted view of women. They are depicted in the most degrading manners possible. It describes the private intimacy of sex, and almost always shows the sexual act as little more than animal behavior.

In his powerful book, *The New American Family*, Jerry Falwell makes this insightful observation about the power of the pornography industry: "At the center of the so-called 'sexual liberation' movement is the highly profitable pornography industry which trades on exploitation and corruption. The clowns of crime laugh all the way to the bank while destroying men, women, and children with equal abandon."[1]

Falwell goes on to observe that there is more and more evidence today demonstrating a close relationship between pornography and sexual crimes. For example, Michigan state police found that pornography is used in 41% of sexual assault cases investigated by the state. In North Carolina, the state police found that 75% of convicted sex offenders had hard-core pornography in their homes or cars.

Pornography is more than just nudity. It commonly displays bizarre perversions of human sexual relationships. Pictures are often shown of women being tortured or mutilated during sex. Some are brutalized with whips, chains, and other instruments of destruction.

The accessibility of pornography is feeding the sexual addictions of millions of Americans who are exposed to the worst kinds of human distortions. Counselors are increasingly encountering people who are addicted to pornography. This sexual epidemic has inflicted this nation with abnormal lives of sexually transmitted disease, marital infidelity, divorce, and sexual child abuse.

The problem of child pornography is so bad that Falwell acknowledges: "There is no way of knowing just how many children are exploited and abused each day in this country, or how these young victims are affected by their involvement."[2]

The corruption of American's morals

Since the publication of the first *Playboy* magazine in 1953, an avalanche of various types of pornography has inundated the shelves of America's convenience stores. Tom Elliff calls it a "sinister attack on America."[3] He observes that 41% of all sex crimes are directly related to the use of pornography. Rape has increased by 700% over the past 30 years, while the pornography industry has blossomed. Ninety percent of all child molesters admit that they first saw what they did displayed in a pornography magazine or portrayed in a movie.

Pornography is now easily accessible in our convenience stores, grocery stores, or even in our homes through cable television. Labeling it "adult" entertainment does not eliminate the fact that it is perversion. Whether adults or young people are watching it doesn't make it any less sinful. Besides, using a label like "adult only" only makes it all the more attractive and alluring to children and young people.

The normalization of homosexuality by the media is now causing the same normalization to occur in relation to the definition of pedophilia. Pedophilia is currently defined as sexual perversion with children as the preferred sexual object. Believe it or not, the American Psychiatric Association has attempted to redefine pedophilia in its revision of *The Diagnostic and Statistical Manual IV*. In it, the APA has redefined the term pedophile to signify a person who merely feels "clinically significant distress" over his condition or feels socially handicapped because of it.

In other words, the APA has opened the door for the normalization of pedophilia! If an individual can molest a child and not feel guilt for his behavior, the APA suggests that he or she should not be considered a pedophile.

The *National Liberty Journal* recently reported that Joseph Nicolosi of the National Association for Research and Therapy of Homosexuality says this new definition has serious consequences for families wanting to protect their children from sexual molesters.[4]

Dr. Nicolosi said the APA's startling new definition of a pedophile proves that the organization is not living up to its responsibility in properly defining what is normal or abnormal.

Dr. James Dobson, of Focus on the Family, has warned: "The normalization of pedophilia is now going through the same process that homosexuality went through in the early 1970's and is being pushed by organized homosexual groups."[5]

In the past, homosexual groups attempted to distance themselves from pedophile organizations in order to encourage the general acceptance of homosexuality as normal behavior. Recently, however, the National Man-Boy Lovers Association

(NAMBLA) has been permitted to participate in several gay events. NAMBLA has been around for years, conducting clandestine meetings in order to allow its members to revel in their lust for young boys.

Homosexual lobbyists have a vested interest in pathologicizing sexual disorders, because once one believes that homosexuality is normal, it is difficult then to draw a clear distinction against pedophilia. In other words, the weakened position that American institutions have taken on the issue of homosexuality is opening the door for homosexuals to make profit of the young people of America!

The new APA definition implies that the individual considered most "healthy" is the one whose pedophilia does not cause him personal distress. By contrast, the individual considered "unhealthy" is the one who would feel some sense of guilt or distress over his homosexual pedophilic orientation. The tragedy of this redefinition is that it attempts to normalize that which the Bible clearly condemns. Many critics predict that the next effort on the part of liberal politicians and homosexual lobbying groups would be lowering the age of consent laws involving homosexual relationships with children.

We can't, we must not, tolerate this kind of perverted behavior! Once any society begins to allow this type of behavior to exist, let alone be legalized, it invites total and absolute disaster. It will only be a matter of time until the homosexual exploitation of children will be so widespread in our society that it will be virtually impossible to prevent it. We have witnessed the changes that have occurred in the public attitude over homosexuality over the past thirty years, and can project thirty more years in the future. It is only a matter of time until almost any imaginable sexual perversion will be legal and acceptable by the standards and definitions of a secular society which has sold its soul to moral degradation.

Child pornography is escalating at a sudden rate in the United States. There are even such things as child seducer's manuals, and playing cards that picture naked children in sexual acts with adults. Child pornography is a vile crime of moral perversion and child abuse. Dr. James Dobson cited one study of eighty civilizations that degenerated to the level of sexual child abuse and all have collapsed socially and politically![6]

The pornographic explosion distorts the Biblical view of women, perverts American youth, and corrupts the moral fiber of society itself. The proliferation of pornography into our society is in itself powerful evidence of the decadence of the American public. The moral fiber of the nation has deteriorated to the point that we can't survive without a drastic reversal of the permissiveness that tolerates pornography in the first place.

Dr. Ted Vath, Professor of Psychiatry at the University of Kansas, recently spoke at the American Family Forum in Washington, D.C. He stated that pornography results in "serious psychological disturbances" for millions of Americans. William Stanmeyer, Professor at the Indiana University School of Law, stated that there is now significant evidence from criminal studies contradicting the liberal claim that there is no link between pornography and crime.

Dr. Gary Hall, a former Olympic gold medalist recently stated: "Children in adolescence are very susceptible to pornography when their principles are not deeply established, and peer pressure is as important as parental approval. Yet it is the 'in thing' to accept pornography, go to 'adult movies' or to watch 'mature TV shows,' and that is what adolescents will do."[7]

Growing tolerance

Despite the concerns of decent Americans who are shocked at the impact of pornography in our society, many are now calling for its toleration by the Christian community. Richard Quededeaux has said: "Pornography is not condoned, yet it does not warrant undue concern: there are worse evils to fight than pornography."[8] Like many theologians who want to reduce legalism in sexual matters, he and others have lowered the flag of biblical morality. Centuries ago, the poet, Dante, wrote: "The hottest places in hell are reserved for those who, in time of great moral crises, maintain their neutrality."

Sexual permissiveness has resulted in venereal disease in epidemic proportions. Lust, stimulated by pornography, has led to adultery, homosexuality, and the breakup of the American family. The Bible reminds us in James 1:13-15: "But every man is tempted, when he is drawn away of his own lust, and enticed.

Then when lust hath conceived, it bringeth forth sin, and sin, when it is finished, bringeth forth death."

Pornography is a cancer that is changing the character of our society. It is time for decent people to speak up and demand that it be stopped. America cannot remain free and strong as long as she is enslaved to the sexual addictions which are promoted by pornography. Those who are focused only on their personal and sensual desires, will never develop the character necessary to resist the destruction of their society. In a permissive society pornography has the same hedonistic attitudes that destroyed ancient Greece and Rome. In fact, the problem of pornography was so great in the Roman Empire that the Apostle Paul said: "It is shameful even to speak of those things which are done by them in secret" (Eph. 5:12).

Today there is an insidious attack against the basic principles of the Christian life. The media and entertainment industry are leading the attack against biblical morality. It is their ultimate goal to undermine the moral fiber of America and justify blatant immorality.

A recent article in *Newsweek* magazine compared the basic beliefs of average Americans to those of the top leaders in the media industry. The results were astonishing:[9]

- Eighty five percent of Americans still believe adultery is wrong. But less that fifty percent of Hollywood executives believed it is wrong.

- Only four percent of all Americans have no religious affiliation. But forty-five percent of the leaders of the media industry acknowledge they have no religious affiliation.

- Seventy-six percent of all Americans believe that homosexuality is morally wrong. But only twenty percent of Hollywood executives believe that it is wrong.

- Over fifty percent of all Americans believe that abortion is wrong. But ninety-seven percent of Hollywood executives believe that it is right.

The Scripture reminds us that "As a man thinketh in his heart, so is he" (Proverbs 23:7). The kind of television programs, movies, videos and other means of entertainment that have come out of Hollywood should not surprise us. The emphasis on sexual immorality, violence, and the demoralization of America's youth are the products of a movie industry which is consumed with lust.

Tom Elliff observes: "Television programming enters our homes and fills our minds with violence, hatred and sexual immorality, attacking our hearts, seeking our demoralization. When we realize how many hours of television is viewed by the average American each week, is it any wonder that America is in a steep moral decline."[10]

Culture wars

There is a real culture war going on in American society today. The battlefield overlaps into various layers of education, the arts, religion, law, and politics. But it is the entertainment industry that is most visibly at the center of the conflict. A half century ago, the motion picture industry was controlled by a production code that assured viewers that people of faith would be portrayed in a positive light. But for the past several years, the entertainment industry has attacked the faith and undermined the value system of Americans. "If you feel strongly about the decline of the entertainment industry, keep the pressure on Hollywood to change," encourages film critic Michael Medved.[11]

Whether we like it or not, the entertainment industry is one of the major influences in shaping the attitudes and opinions of most Americans. Too many people are developing their morals and values from the influence of films, rather than from Biblical principles. Josh McDowell has observed that even Christian parents are no longer trying to decide the difference between what he calls right from wrong.[12] McDowell lists the tragic impact of the degradation of the American society upon its young people. He notes that the following happens every day in America!

- 2,000 unwed teenaged girls become pregnant.
- 1,106 teenaged girls get abortions.

- 4,219 teenagers contract sexually transmitted diseases.
- 500 adolescents begin using drugs.
- 1,000 adolescents begin drinking alcohol.
- Over 100,000 kids bring guns or weapons to school.
- 3,610 teenagers are assaulted.
- 2,200 teens drop out of high school.
- 100 teenaged girls are raped.
- 6 teens commit suicide.

Notice again that these statistics tell us what happens every single day in the lives of America's teenagers.

Journalist Rowland Methaway has said:

Many of today's youth don't seem to know right from wrong. Children are robbing, maiming, and killing on whims, with no pity and no remorse.[13]

McDowell's survey is even more disturbing when applied to Christian teenagers. In a national survey of church-attending teens, he found the following results:

- 66% lied to a parent, teacher or other adult.
- 59% lied to their peers.
- 35% watched MTV at least once during the past week.
- 36% cheated on an exam.
- 23% smoked a cigarette.
- 20% tried to physically hurt someone.
- 12% got drunk.
- 8% used illegal, nonprescription drugs.

While Christian teens rated better in every category than nonchurched youth, still the fact remains they were involved in questionable practices which contradicted their Christian profession.

The culture war is being lost at the teenage level. New studies indicate that today's generation of young people, often referred to as Generation X, are less interested in spiritual matters, have a lower interest in the Bible, and come from homes in which there is a higher divorce rate than any generation of young people has ever had to deal with in the history of our nation. Josh McDowell observes:

> Our problem goes far deeper than the easy availability of guns or drugs; it defies conventional programs and social solutions. I believe it is a problem that will never be resolved until we identify its source and deal with its root causes.[14]

When anyone complains about the impact of the media industry on society, someone will inevitably shout: "Censorship!" But as former Education Secretary, Bill Bennett, co-director of Empower America has stated: "You're not talking about censorship, you're talking about citizenship!"[15] And I might add, we are talking about the moral health of our nation.

The AIDS epidemic

AIDS was first diagnosed in 1981. It is a disease which attacks the immune system, thus the name Acquired Immunity Deficiency Syndrome, or AIDS. The virus which produces this condition is called HIV, human immuno deficiency virus. It is the virus (HIV) which results in the condition (AIDS).

Once a person is infected with HIV, he or she may live for up to ten years. But eventually the HIV virus results in AIDS, by which the immune system is totally destroyed. The individual eventually dies by contracting basic diseases such as pneumonia, or even the common cold.

It is estimated there are over one million AIDS cases in the U.S. alone. We are the leading nation in all the world carrying the disease of AIDS. While AIDS has been spread rapidly through the sexually promiscuous homosexual community, it is not limited to that community. Any sexually promiscuous person runs the risk of catching the HIV virus, and eventually developing AIDS. In Africa, where AIDS apparently originated, it is known that one out of three women have AIDS. Because AIDS became a prominent problem within the homosexual community, it has become a political hot potato!

Homosexual groups have lobbied the government for relaxed standards in the treatment of those infected with the disease. This year our government will spend nearly 500 million dollars funding the "safe sex" program, but there is no such thing as safe sex outside of marriage. Some have called the government program of a national distribution of condoms to insure the prevention of AIDS as a farce. First of all, condoms are only effective as a contraceptive 84% of the time. Unfortunately, the AIDS virus is 450 times smaller than sperm. So the possibility of AIDS-infected sperm leaking through a condom is incredibly high. Some have actually referred to the condom approach of AIDS prevention as "condom roulette."

AIDS can be spread homosexually and heterosexually. It can result from the body fluid exchange which occurs in sexual intercourse, but it can also be transmitted through IV drug use, drug transfusions, and prenatally from an infected mother to her infant.

The great tragedy of our time is that while this epidemic could potentially be curtailed, our government has listened to the voices of those special interest groups who are determined to protect their own immoral life-styles. Instead of generally encouraging sexual abstinence as a means of restricting the spread of AIDS, government leaders have promoted a disastrous campaign under the misguided term "safe sex."

There is no nation on the face of the earth that has been blessed as much as the United States. But there is no nation more in danger of internal moral destruction than America. We stand at a great crossroads today. The battle for the soul of America is already being waged, and we are losing that battle! If we do not raise our voices now and demand that the American public policy be reversed in the matter of pornography and the spread of sexually explicit materials, our nation is destined to destruction. If that means financial boycotts, public protests, and preaching out against the corruption of our nation's morals, then let us raise our voices like a trumpet and shout it from the housetops!

"Many teenagers get curious
after listening to music that
incorporates drug experiences and
turn to songs created essentially
for drug users."

—Jay Strack
Evangelist

Chapter 4

Drugs
Overcoming the Chemical Curtain

We live in a society which is consumed with alcohol and drugs. Drug abuse is nothing new. It has been a problem for several years, but it is now at epidemic proportions and cannot be overlooked. Drugs came on the public scene in the 1970's and seemed to fade somewhat in the 1980's. However, during the 1980's cocaine replaced heroin as the most serious drug of choice by drug abusers. In the 1990's we are faced with a whole new wave of marijuana usage by teenagers in particular, and many of them idolize the 1970's and are attempting to reintroduce the life-style that was associated with it.

Almost everyone agrees that drugs are a major problem in the United States, yet hardly anyone has a solution for dealing with the problem. Our government officials have waged what they have called a "war on drugs," but it has been more like a minor scrimmage than a war. We hardly have the drug lords on the run. The pushers and promoters of drugs openly function within our society. Laws designed to limit drug abuse are often not enforced effectively. Kids have little respect for those laws and believe that they will never be held accountable for their behavior.

The drug epidemic is so serious that it is destroying the next generation. Just when our public officials thought they had turned the corner on the problem, it has reemerged more powerful and more devastating than ever before.

Jay Strack is a former drug user who was converted during the hippie movement. Jay is now a renowned Baptist evangelist and recently served as vice president of the Southern Baptist Convention. In his book, Drugs and Drinking, Jay makes several observations to help us understand the seriousness of this problem.[1] Strack suggests there are three categories of drug users in America.

First are the occasional users. This could include anyone from teenagers to housewives to young professionals.

Second are the thrill seekers. These are usually high school and college-aged young people who use drugs for the thrill of it. Some of them are weekend users or party-types whose drug use may get out of control.

Third are the drug addicts. The addicts' entire life revolves around the drug scene and its related experiences. He or she exhibits psychological dependence (habituation) and physical dependence (addiction). The National Institute of Mental Health estimates that drugs will cost the addict anywhere from 15 to 20 years of his expected lifespan.

If drugs are so dangerous, why are they such a turn on for so many people? Millions of American teenagers experiment with drugs every year! Strack suggests five reasons why drugs have such an alluring temptation for teenagers:

1. **Pressure.**
One of the greatest needs teenagers face is that of acceptance. As they struggle to develop through adolescence to young adulthood, most teens feel they're different, rejected, or left out. The desire for popularity and acceptance will often cause them to pull away from their family values and spiritual heritage, even

at the expense of their own safety, because they feel pressured by other teenagers to give in to the temptation of drugs.

2. Escape.

Millions of Americans are looking for an escape from the pressures of life. Some of them get into drugs because they feel restless or confused about themselves. Others turn to drugs because they feel bored and neglected. There may be millions of reasons why people may feel the need to escape from the pressures of life, but the desire to escape is one of the major reasons teens are attracted to drugs. Escaping the pressures of home, school, dating, and even the physiological changes of life are enough to drive kids to look for a way to escape, and drugs offer them that escape.

3. Availability.

The easy access of drugs to our young people is almost unbelievable. Every teenage hangout and restroom in public school is a source of drug availability. Kids don't have to look very far to find drugs. Recent surveys indicate that 60% of high school seniors acknowledged that they had tried marijuana. A recent Gallup Poll found that over 80% of their high schools respondents indicated that marijuana was readily available to them.[2]

4. Curiosity.

Most kids experiment with drugs because of basic curiosity. They are curious to know what the experience is really like. Many of them try to act "cool" and find that drugs is a way to gain acceptance they otherwise could not find. Strack observes:

Many teenagers get curious after listening to music that incorporates drug experiences and turn to songs created essentially for drug users.[3]

Such misguided curiosity has led many a young person to personal disaster. Thinking they would discover some wonderful experience in life, they found themselves addicted to the very drugs they had thought would bring them a new sense of personal freedom. The tragedy is that our society allows the promotion of drug abuse to go unhindered in many cases. The rap music industry is filled with drug-related references and no one has taken the time to confront this issue and demand that the entertainment industry do something about it.

Who's to blame for the drug problem in America? It's not the kids! It is not even the drug growers and producers. The real blame ought to be laid at the feet of those who have blatantly and openly promoted its usage to our young people. The singers and songwriters who glorify drug use are to be blamed. The radio stations that play their music ought to be blamed, and the advertisers who are making their living off the music which promotes drug use are also to be blamed. It is time we laid the blame of responsibility at the place where it really rests!

5. Emptiness.

One of the ultimate reasons people turn to drugs is because of their own personal and spiritual and psychological emptiness. The epidemic of drugs, the rash of suicide attempts, and the broken lives of young people are seen all over the landscape of America. Kids are turning to drugs and alcohol to alleviate the loneliness, depression and anger that they feel inside. With a 50% divorce rate, there are millions of kids who feel rejected by their parents.

The alcoholic atmosphere of America

Our nation is overrun with excessive alcoholism. Alcohol is definitely a drug! It is certainly a "gateway" drug which leads to other drug problems. 98% of all drug addicts acknowledge that their dependency problems began with alcohol. Alcohol is also the #1 killer of young people between the ages of 15 and 24. Three-fourths of all adult problem drinkers acknowledge they started drinking as teenagers. Every 5 minutes an American teenager is arrested for a drug or alcohol offense: over 80,000 per year. Every 30 minutes an American teenager is arrested for drunk driving: nearly 20,000 per year.

Alcohol and drug abuse cause the greatest danger to our nation's health, social, and legal problems. Much of the wanton divorce rate can be blamed on excessive drug and alcohol usage.

Millions of parents consume alcohol on a daily basis. It is estimated that 70% of our nation's homes have alcohol in them. The standard family lecture on not drinking falls on deaf ears when the refrigerator is filled with beer and liquor, and the medicine cabinet is packed with a lot of unnecessary "legal drugs." In spite of the so-called "war on drugs," there's been a marked increase in drug overdoses and drug-related problems. Those numbers have tripled in the last ten years.

Cocaine-related deaths have more than doubled during the same period of time. Statistics released by the National Institute on Drug Abuse (NIDA) indicate that America's teenagers continue to show the highest level of drug use of young people any where in the world![4]

Alcohol is the most widely used psychoactive drug in America. The National Council on Alcoholism estimates there are more than ten million alcoholics in the United States. It is also estimated that almost 70% of Americans drink some kind of alcohol on a weekly basis. Alcoholism is so widespread that it is the nation's third largest health problem, following heart disease and cancer. It afflicts ten million people, costs 60 billions dollars, and is implicated in nearly 200,000 deaths every year. Alcohol is the contributing factor in 50% of all automobile-related deaths, 67% of murders, and 33% of all suicides.

Despite the seriousness of alcoholism, our society continues to want to believe that alcohol is really not a drug. Our television sets are filled with advertisements promoting alcohol and the "good life." It is ironic that the National Health Institute has convinced us of the dangers of cigarette smoking to the point that it has been almost eliminated from public places in our nation. Yet, we continue to drink ourselves to death! Until America takes alcohol seriously, we will never solve our drug and alcohol dependence problem! There is an old Japanese proverb that says:

"First, the man takes a drink,
Then, the drink takes the man!"

The drugging of America

The chemical quotient that is found across this nation affects millions of Americans every single day. Many begin by experimenting with marijuana, but soon move on to more serious drugs. Occasional users often become serious drug addicts.

Marijuana

Marijuana is the most common drug used in the United States today. While many have attempted to minimize its dangers, its usage has drugged an entire generation of young people. Marijuana is a drug found in the leaves of the Indian hemp plant (cannabis sativa). These flowers have the highest PSC resin of any plants in the world. The drug is popularly called pot, tea, hemp, grass, or weed. The butt of a marijuana cigarette is referred to as a roach. The grasslike product is usually rolled into a homemade cigarette called a "joint." Strack observes that the smoke from a marijuana joint is harsh, but sweet, and is often unrecognized by adults. That is why it is possible for a teenager to be able to use marijuana excessively and not be caught by his parents.

Cocaine

Once called the "rich man's drug", cocaine is now the drug of daily choice for nearly 5 million Americans. Despite its popularity and use by doctors, athletes, and rock stars, cocaine remains a serious psychoactive drug that destroys the central nervous system. It produces an artificial sense of restlessness and energy and a false sense of intense euphoria. Cocaine raises the body's blood pressure, constricts the circulatory system, and increases the heart rate. For that reason, heart attacks are a common side affect of excessive cocaine use.

Why do people use cocaine? The same reason they use other drugs — to escape from the pressures of life. An added attraction of cocaine is that it gives one an artificial sense of superiority. Therefore actors, athletes, and other performers feel it can give them the "high" they need in order to accomplish their tasks.

The tragedy of cocaine abuse is it is one of the most addictive drugs available in America today. Some have suggested that they have little hope for the excessive cocaine user. Dr. Mitchell Rosenthal of the Phoenix House Drug Treatment House has said: "Of all the drugs, cocaine is the most difficult to deal with."[5] Several professional athletes have recently ruined their entire careers because of cocaine addiction.

LSD

LSD is the most potent psychedelic drug. LSD is short for lysergic acid diethylamide. Lysergic acid comes from ergot, the famous rye grain. In Medieval Europe it was referred to as "St. Anthony's Fire" because the blackened toes and fingers of those who ignorantly ate contaminated grain appeared to be charred. Strack notes that some categorize LSD as a hallucinogen because it causes hallucinations and even temporary insanity. Others call it a psychedelic because it produces self-transcendence and mystical experiences.[6]

The tragedy of LSD is that it destroys, disrupts, and disorganizes mental activity. Rather than expand the mind, it ultimately destroys the mind. The "so-called" turn on from LSD is ultimately a turn off! The greatest drawback to LSD is its own unpredictability. Every "trip" can lead to excitement or a terrifying personal experience. LSD is also known to call depression, anxiety, and psychotic breakdowns. One of its most harmful effects is that of "flash backs." Those who were hurt by LSD use may experience reoccurrence of flash- backs for several months afterwards.

PCP

PCP is often called "angel dust." PCP is a veterinary anesthetic known as phencyclidine and sold under the trade name "Sernyl." Even as an animal tranquilizer it is often mixed with other drugs because it is considered too dangerous, even for animals. When Rodney King was arrested, he was on PCP and responded violently toward the officers who were attempting to subdue him.

Street chemists make PCP cheaply and easily. The drug can be manufactured by anyone with a minimum knowledge of chemistry and a few pieces of equipment. Five hundred dollars worth of chemicals can be made into angel dust worth at least two hundred thousand dollars. PCP is a white crystalline powder that can be smoked, injected, or taken as a liquid or tablet. Many chemists mix PCP with LSD and sell it to unsuspecting teenagers who assume it is a milder drug. Tragically, PCP holds its users in a state of depression and addiction which often leads to suicide.

Stimulants

Stimulants are drugs that act to stimulate the central nervous system. The most commonly used stimulants are amphetamines, known on the street as "uppers," "speed," or "crystals."

Some observers claim that 50% of the 50 trillion amphetamine tablets produced in the United States annually are sold illegally on our city streets and in our public schools. Speed can be swallowed, inhaled, snorted, or injected with a needle. When drug users begin "shooting up" with amphetamines, this produces a result referred to as a "rush." Once the addict begins injecting the drug, he has taken a serious step toward lifelong drug addiction via needles.

Sedatives

Sedatives or "downers" are various forms of barbiturates. Generally in the form of capsules, they relax the central nervous system. The danger of barbiturates is that they can cause brain damage by cutting down on the amount of oxygen necessary to reach the brain cells. Death is caused by respiratory depression and cardiac arrest. One can even go so far as to bring about his or her own suicide by an overdose of barbiturates or "sleeping pills."

Barbiturates kill more users of legal and illegal drugs than any other type of overdose in America today. They also kill as many adults as they do teenagers. In many ways, "downers" are the drug of choice of America's adult generation.

Heroin

Heroin is a member of the opium family and is a white crystalline powder derived from morphine. Popularly known as "smack" or "junk", heroin is the most addicting of all drugs.

Heroin is generally injected with a needle and results in a psychological high we call a "fix." Excessive heroin addiction eventually leads to premature death. When it is injected intravenously with a hypodermic needle, this is commonly referred to as "mainlining." The crystals are measured in a teaspoon, dissolved in water, and "pricked" with a match or candle. The liquid is then drawn into a needle through a ball of cotton and then injected into the arm. Heroin addiction results in the shakes, vomiting, diarrhea, muscle spasms, delusions, and terrifying hallucinations.

Because of the high cost of heroin, the addict usually turns to a life of crime in order to pay for his excessive habit. The tragedy of heroin addiction is that it is the end result of a long line of addictive practices on the part of drug users and inevitably results in their deaths. This is further complicated by the potential of passing and receiving AIDS through hypodermic injections. The combination of the use of needles and highly addictive drugs is literally killing a generation of American drug addicts.

Drugproofing America

The time has come for sensible Americans to stand up against the drug problems of our nation. We must declare real war on drugs! And we must do it now! I believe that concerned Americans have talked about these problems for the better part of the past twenty years without developing adequate solutions. We cannot sacrifice the next generation like we did the last one!

You don't kill a rattlesnake by gently tapping it on the head. You get an axe and chop its head off! You get a sledge hammer and bludgeon it to death! This may sound harsh, tough language to some, but it is nothing compared to the tragic damage the drugs are doing to our young people. I love the youth of American far more than I do the drug-trafficker who is trying to get rich at the expense of our nation's young people.

Stricter laws

The Christian community needs to appeal to our politicians for stricter legislation against the promotion, selling, and distribution of illegal drugs. We need much stricter law enforcement against drug pushers, users, and distributors. I am convinced that many young people are not afraid to try drugs because they do not fear our nation's legal or judicial system. They know that we do not mean business and they are taking every advantage of it. The time has come to show them that we really do mean business, even if it means some stiff penalties for "innocent" users. We cannot wait until there is a lull in drug usage in order to enforce stricter penalties. There never will be such a lull. Drug use is only going to continue to accelerate until we determine to stop it.

We need to enact much stronger penalties against the major drug producers and distributors. Criminal offenses may need to be tightened even to the point of capital punishment, if necessary. We must cut off the serpent's head before it poisons us all! We need stronger enforcement of prison terms with less exceptions. Every time our court suspends sentences, lowers penalties and allows quick and easy parole, they only encourage the problem to get worse. I believe with all my heart that we need a president, congress, and judicial system that will do whatever is necessary to win this war.

One of the great frustrations of those of us who fought in Vietnam was the fact that our government never determined to win that war. Many gave their lives, their blood, and those like myself gave their limbs! We did it because we believed that it was a war worth winning, yet we were not backed up by those at the highest levels of government who were determined to stand with us in that commitment. The same exact thing is going to happen in the so-called "war against drugs" if we do not determine to win this war at all costs. This is no time for hesitation. This is no time for neutrality. We must act now to encourage our legislators to declare an all-out war that will lead to victory over the drug problem in this nation.

Stronger youth ministries

Anyone who has ever worked with young people will tell you that they must have the encouragement and reinforcement of their peers. This means that our churches need to provide stronger youth ministries which are aimed at helping build up our teenagers. We must do everything we can in the church to help drugproof the Christian family. Coming to services alone will not accomplish that, no matter how wonderful the services may be. Our young people need the reassurance that we love them and generally care about them. We need to help walk them through the difficult adjustments of adolescence. If there's any place that they need to feel loved and accepted, it is in our Christian homes and our Christian churches.

We also need to provide positive alternatives for our kids. Many young people become attracted to drugs because they do not have anything positive filling their lives. For some, there is a spiritual vacuum. They need a personal relationship with Jesus Christ who can fill that vacuum and give them meaning and purpose for living. For others, there is the struggle of self-acceptance. Even some of our Christian teens feel rejected or unappreciated by their peers. We need to encourage the kind of youth ministries that will hold the standard of Christian living high, and yet be willing to reach down to the lowest level of those who are struggling to know where they fit in the Christian adolescent community. Those kids need our love and encouragement just as much as anyone else — perhaps even more so.

We need to teach our kids to stand alone against temptation. We need to be straightforward and honest in helping them understand that we realize that they are living in a drug and alcohol-saturated society. We cannot assume that, because a teenager is a Christian or a member of the church or its youth ministry, he will be oblivious to the temptation of drugs and alcohol. Our kids need to realize that they will be approached by other teens and offered drugs and alcohol. We need to help them understand the seriousness of the situation and give them the spiritual tools and equipment to withstand the onslaught of temptation.

Parental example

One of the most practical steps that any one us can take is making sure that we are setting the right example in our own homes. Parents who drink are hypocritical if they think they are going to convince their children not to drink. Parents who are quick to overuse prescription drugs for every little ache or pain they have are foolish if they think their kids are not going to be susceptible to illegal drugs. Addiction begins in the mind, and only later expresses itself in physical actions.

Most addicts are the product of a home in which there is a great deal of negative thinking, parental neglect, and spiritual emptiness. Our families need to become models of spiritual integrity, genuine love, and parental concern. If your family is uncommunicative and silent, chances are your children will feel lonely and isolated. If there is a great deal of spiritual abuse or neglect, your children will probably grow up rejecting the beliefs and values that you have as parents. That is why it is so important that you set the example in every area for your children.

It is also important that our kids really believe that we love them and care about them. We may not always understand the depth of their struggles, and they may not understand (or appreciate) the intensity of our concerns, but if they know in their hearts that we really want God's best for them, they will always respect us.

It has often been said: "No one cares how much you know, until they know how much you care." And that is true of teenagers just as much as it is of adults.

"Therefore, to hold human nature in check, God has ordained human government to protect, maintain and sustain human life."

—Dr. Ed Hindson

Chapter 5

Crime
Let's Stop the Violence

Violent crime has become the major problem in American society. According to the FBI, the rate of violent crime in the United States is worse than any other country in the world. A murder occurs every 21 minutes, a rape every 5 minutes, a robbery every 45 seconds, and aggravated assault every 29 seconds. At the same time, juvenile crime has increased 60% from 1980 to 1990.

The crime crisis is worse among minorities and the poor, but it is out of control at virtually every level of society. Yet, while the number of crimes is increasing, the Republicans' Contract with America indicates that "a small percentage of criminals commit the vast majority of violent crimes."[1] A 1991 study done by the Bureau of Alcohol, Tobacco, and Firearms (ATF) indicated that 471 hard criminals had a total of 3,088 convictions. That is an average of six-and-a-half felonies each. To make matters worse, some of these criminals are repeat offenders. 30% of all the murders in America are committed by people on probation, parole, or bail. To remedy this situation, the Contract with America calls for "truth in sentencing" laws which require criminals to serve a longer portion of their sentence and a "three-strikes-you're-out" law aimed at repeat offenders.

The Justice Department estimates there are more people in prison in the United States than ever before - - 528,945 inmates in federal and state institutions. The FBI claims that 74% of those released from prison will be back within 4 years. It has already cost the American government an average of $17,324 annually to keep someone in prison. New prison construction runs between $60,000 to $80,000 per cell.

It is time for America to wake up and get its head out of the sand. You cannot continue to allow violent crime to run unheeded in the streets of our nation. In Biblical times, the Scripture indicted the nation of Israel because "violence filled the land." It is almost impossible to get someone to roll their window down and stop and give you directions any longer when you're driving a car. If you stop and speak to someone on the sidewalk, they look startled. We all feel unsafe because of the illogical murder and violence which has struck at the very heart and core of our society. We live in an unsafe society.

Our nation's capital has the strongest gun laws in America, and yet has the highest murder rate per capita of any other city in this country. It's not guns, knives, or weapons; it is human behavior that is the problem. The wickedness and violence in our society is sounding the death knell of America's own funeral. We are watching ourselves die. What really bothers me is that some people don't even seem to care! I've never seen such apathy, even among Christians, regarding the serious state of affairs in our nation.

But thank God, many of them are aroused to do something about the seriousness of these problems. I realize that many of us say to ourselves that we cannot solve the problem of violent crime alone, but we can all use our voices to speak out against it, and demand that our elected officials deal with this problem effectively. Every time you vote in an election, you are not only selecting a candidate, but you are choosing a political and social platform. You are voting for the future agenda of America, and if we continue to put people into office who do not take seriously the matter of stopping violent crime, we will never see the end to such crimes, yet if we would vote only for those who are *willing* to do something to turn this situation around, we can see it changed immediately.

The issue is not gun control

The Second Amendment to the Constitution of the United States guarantees the right to bear arms. This is no less necessary today than it was in 1791. I personally have a number of guns in my own home, and I believe in the freedom and the necessity of protecting my own home against criminals. Since adopting a virtual handgun ban, Washington, D.C. has recorded an increase of almost 200% in its murder rate. It is now the nation's #1 murder capitol. Criminals are the problem, not guns. Criminals are responsible for crime, guns are not. The day you give up your guns, criminals will still have theirs.

The problem has never been the guns; the problem has always been the human heart. Beyond that, the liberal agenda of legislatures and judicial officials will never be able to change the crime rate in America by merely attempting to ban guns.

The right to own guns does not mean one desires to use one. It merely means that we have the right to protect ourselves if and when necessary. I hope that it will never be necessary for me to use one, yet I reserve the right to be able to do so if it ever is necessary.

Too many times, the liberal politicians in our country have tried to resolve the crime problem by suggesting that we need better prisons, more social welfare programs, and loosened restrictions on the sentencing of criminals. These things will never solve the problem of serious crime in America.

The Republicans Contract with America calls for the authorization of funds to prosecute capital cases. The Taking Back our Streets Act authorizes equal funding for states to prosecute cases that involve the death penalty. They are also calling for reform of the death penalty procedures. The act mandates that juries be instructed to recommend a death sentence if aggravating circumstances do not have mitigating factors.

No one wants to see innocent people punished unnecessarily, but we have gone to such extremes to avoid that possibility that we are letting criminals walk the streets free of any fear of reprisal from our government. When a person can be convicted of murder, admit that he committed the murder, and still be sitting in prison 15 to 20 years later, there is something wrong with our legal, judicial, and penal system.

Those who object to the death penalty will always argue that it is wrong to take another life, but the Bible tells us very clearly that we are to hold men responsible for their actions, especially in the area of the taking of human life (Genesis 9:6).

The Contract with America also calls for mandatory minimum sentencing for drug crimes. While some argue that mandatory sentencing hinders the judge from considering the nature of a given offense, nevertheless, it sends a strong signal to criminals that they will serve a minimum sentence if they commit certain crimes. Prosecutors see this as a necessary step in serious law enforcement. The Taking Back our Streets Act establishes a mandatory minimum sentence of ten years for the use of a gun in committing a violent crime, and it is increased to twenty years for a second conviction, and life for a third conviction. This Act also mandates that criminals pay full restitution to their victims for damages caused as a result of that crime.[2]

The basic problem with previous congressional crime bills is that they are loaded down with long-ineffective social welfare programs. Two-thirds of state prison inmates have been convicted of a violent crime. Crime rates soar as a result of the system's inability to rehabilitate offenders. Serious enforcement of punishment against violent criminals is not an overreaction which eliminates the rights of criminals. It is common sense approach to dealing with criminals which is absolutely necessary in a nation in which prisoners can sue prison officials for "cruel and unusual punishment" because they lack frisbees, art supplies and chunky-styled peanut butter! These cases cost the courts millions of dollars in resources and could be resolved through administrative matters, rather than resorting to federal lawsuits.

A return to sanity

We must urge our legislatures to take seriously the whole issue of violent crime. I'm not calling for Christians to brutalize any element of society, but it is time that we dealt seriously with those who have already brutalized society. Those who object to strict penalties will always cry out for the rights of prisoners, while overlooking the rights of the victims! If you could spend an evening in a police car, as I have done, and watch our law enforcement officers attempting to deal with violent crime in our nation's major cities, you would be terrified. Rapes, robbery and murder are commonplace events, occurring almost nightly. One need only turn on the evening news in his local city and listen to the run down of violent crimes that have occurred that day. These things don't happen just by coincidence. They are the result of a society that has abandoned God; a society that has turned its back on moral values; a society that has been convinced there are no moral absolutes. Once we pull the moral and spiritual rug out from under any group of people, they will resort to animal-like behavior.

Our schools teach our children that they are animals who have evolved from other animals, that there are no absolute moral standards, and that there is no God, heaven, or hell. Left in such a moral and spiritual vacuum, these kids grow up thinking it does not matter what one does in regard to his or her own personal behavior.

Where there is no God, there is no law. Once you remove God-consciousness from society, it will be replaced by brute force. Whoever controls the police or the army will automatically control the society. All public debate of moral and social behavior ceases. The powerful rule by the right of power alone. It is for these very reasons that our founding fathers wrote into the fabric of this great nation the principles of right and wrong, based on a Judeo-Christian belief system.

Tim LaHaye expresses it this way:

> Our present dilemma finds the secularizers — that's 6% of those who don't believe in anyone's God or religion — maintain a virtual stranglehold on public education.[3]

Law and law enforcement go hand in hand. Ever since the Garden of Eden, the sword has been the symbol of strength. Satan himself is described in scripture as provoking the lawless spirit of disobedience. "Therefore, the sinful nature of man is in conflict with the laws of God. It is the source of individual and corporate evil in society that must be restrained by law.

The ultimate condition which results from lawlessness is chaos and anarchy. It is in this state that evil dominates society. Ed Dobson and Ed Hindson have observed:

> Therefore, to hold human nature in check, God has ordained human government to protect, maintain and sustain human life.[4]

Christian writers like St. Augustine believed that government was necessary to inhibit evil and promote the common good of all men. R.C. Sproul explains:

> By that he meant that government itself is made necessary by the fact of evil, and even though governments may be oppressive and exploited and corrupt, the worst government is still better than no government.[5]

The biblical passage on the responsibility of the Christian to human government is found in Romans 13:1-7. Here the believer is admonished to respect the authority of human government. Dobson and Hindson suggest the following five steps to that process:[6]

1. Political authority is ordained by God.

The Apostle Paul wrote: "The powers that be are ordained of God" (13:1). Therefore, all human authority is delegated subject to the delegator, who is God. The power of government is a God-given authority in our lives.

2. Obedience is a religious obligation.

The believer is commanded to obey civil authority and not to resist "the ordinance of God" (13:2). The Christian is to do all he can to obey the law and live peaceably with all men. However, his obedience is one of testimony, not blind obligation.

3. Government exists to promote justice.

Paul viewed the magistrate as a "minister of God" to whom honor is due. By this he acknowledged the responsibility of the

CRIME: LET'S STOP THE VIOLENCE

government to protect its citizenry and promote the common good. Government is to be God's instrument of maintaining justice in society and restraining evil.

4. Resistance will be judged.

The Scripture warns that resisting the authority of government is tantamount to resisting the authority of God, who ordained it. This passage assumes that government will be just. It is not a command to submit to tyranny or injustice. But it is a reminder that injustices will not be tolerated within the proper sphere of governmental authority.

5. Hierarchy of ethics.

As Christians we are obligated to obey the government. In the scripture we are obligated to obey God. Whenever the two appear to conflict with one another, the believer must put spiritual values over civil authorities. For example, if you are told to deny Christ, as were many early Christians, you must disobey government in order to obey Christ's command not to deny Him before men. (See Acts 5:29).

In a free democratic society like the United States, this has rarely ever been a problem. However, with the increased secularization of our society it could certainly become a problem in the future. The early church was often caught in this dilemma between the authority of the church and the power of the Roman Empire. Standing upon their Christian beliefs and principles, they chose to suffer and die, if necessary, rather than compromise their beliefs.

To the Christian, Christ is the Lord of Life. Therefore, He is the ultimate authority in both earthly and heavenly matters. True Christianity departs from crusading medieval Catholicism or militant Islamic fanatics, because it recognizes that the Gospel cannot be spread by the sword. Christ's kingdom can only be advanced by its acceptance into the willing hearts of men and women.

You cannot and dare not force people to become Christians. To do so would defeat our own purpose. Whenever people accept a belief system because it is forced upon them against their will, it will only ultimately fail. But that does not mean that as Christians we have no opinion or responsibility in regard to the enforcement of democratic public policy.

We have a wonderful privilege of living in the greatest nation on earth. It is a free nation. It is a society that allows anyone or everyone the opportunity to speak his conscience and stand up for his or her beliefs. It is also a society that does not punish those who disagree with us simply because they disagree. But when it comes to the matter of civil obedience, the Bible is clear that God has ordained human governments to maintain law and order in society. The depletion of our legal, judicial, and criminal enforcement system is a slap in the very face of God! The liberal politicians have taken it upon themselves to try to run this country without God, and that will never work!

You cannot have justice without a recognition of that which is just. The Bible makes it clear there is only one who is ultimately just — and that is God. Once we educate and legislate Him out of our lives and out of our society, we will be left with anarchy and chaos. It is for this very reason that we are now struggling with this whole issue of violent crime in America today. Secular educators have taught our young people they are no more than glorified animals, and so they are acting like it! Violent crimes among teenagers is at an all-time high, not only in America, but in the history of the world! You cannot sit back and simply hope that things will get better. They will not! Things will get worse - much worse!

What has caused this dramatic change in our American society in the past 30 years? I'm convinced it is the end result of the foothold secular humanism has gained in our educational institutions. We have convinced ourselves that we don't need God or His rules, standards, and principles. Secularists are trying to organize society on the basic and fundamental belief that man is inherently good. Denying the biblical doctrine of human depravity, they have foolishly assumed that most people want to do what is right. Therefore, they recommend a relaxed approach to enforcement of criminal statutes. Assuming that criminals are merely the victims of their social circumstances, they foolishly recommend more high-cost social welfare programs to resolve the problem, but we have been spending money on welfare for more than 50 years now with no appreciable results. Things have not gotten better, they are worse than they have ever been!

The time has come for Christians to raise their voice in support of those who are calling for stronger methods of dealing with the outburst of criminals activity which has overrun this nation. We cannot wait for liberal politicians to resolve this problem. I'm convinced that nothing short of a clean sweep in both houses of Congress will bring about the kind of immediate and dramatic change that is necessary in this country. The Contract with America called for such change in the elections of 1994. This was certainly a step in the right direction, and we have already seen some of their changes enacted, yet in order for this to become what it needs to be, we need another dramatic sweeping change in the political elections of 1996. I, for one, believe that every Christian has a responsibility to vote his conscience and convictions during local, state, and national elections. You cannot simply sit back and condemn the current situation. It is easier to curse the darkness than to light a candle, yet we must light the candle of truth and justice if America is to have a chance to remain the free and vibrant nation she has always been.

We have actually convinced
ourselves that slogans will save us.
Shoot up if you must, but use a
clean needle. Enjoy sex whenever
and with whomever you wish, but
wear a condom. No! The answer
is no! Not because it isn't cool or
smart, or because you might end
up in jail or dying in an AIDS
ward. But no because it's wrong!

—Ted Koppel
Nightline

Chapter 6

Homosexuality
Our National Perversion

Homosexuality is one of the most controversial subjects in our nation today. The Bible clearly condemns it as a sin against the very nature and purpose of God. Despite this, our national media continues to promote it as nothing more than an "alternative life-style." The tragedy is that this so-called alternative is destroying the moral fabric of our nation.

God's verdict on homosexuality is absolutely clear in scripture. Old Testament law forbids adultery in any form, and protects sexual morality and integrity of marriage. Old Testament law, as expressed in the Book of Leviticus, expands on the Ten Commandments and clearly says: "You shall not lie with a man as with a woman; it is an abomination" (Lev. 18:22). The Scripture further states: "If a man lies with a male as with a woman, both of them have committed an abomination: they shall be put to death. Their bloodguiltiness is upon them" (Lev. 20:13).

Even before the law was given, God made it clear from the very beginning that He created the human race "male and female." God Himself established the first marriage and that marriage was between Adam and Eve - not Adam and Steve or

77

Madam and Eve! Greg Bahnsen notes: "The creation of sexual differentiation by God from the beginning established heterosexuality as the normative direction for the sexual impulse and act."[1]

Later in the Book of Genesis, we read the story of the destruction of Sodom and Gomorrah in Genesis 19. When the two angelic visitors came into the city of Sodom, they were met by Lot who encouraged them to stay in his home for fear of their safety. When the sodomites sought to "know" them, they were requesting a homosexual relationship with them. Lot opposed their desire and called it a "great wickedness" (v.6-7). The city of Sodom was totally destroyed by God because it was overrun with the sin of homosexual debauchery.

The New Testament condemns the sin of the sodomites in 2 Peter 2:8 and Jude 7, referring to it as "lawless behavior" which resulted in "going after strange flesh." The biblical term in the Greek is *sarkos heteras*, "different flesh." It was an unnatural sexual desire that dominated the atmosphere and led to the severity of God's judgment upon it. The Apostle Paul refers to homosexual activity as "degrading passions" for which reason God abandons homosexuals to "committing indecent acts" (Romans 1:28-31). Bahnsen adds: "Homosexuality exchanges the natural use of sex for unnatural sexual practices, thereby evidencing immoral perversion in the most intimate of human relations, and 'worthy of death.'"[2]

A moral crusade

We need to call for a moral crusade against the establishment of homosexuality as a legitimate life-style and an acceptable minority within the United States. Homosexuals, sodomites, lesbians, and other perverts have no right to have more rights than the average taxpaying citizens. The Bible clearly states that homosexuality is perverted, reprobate and unnatural. If they ever turn America into another Sodom, you can mark it down that God's judgment will fall on this nation!

Homosexuals do not qualify as a minority and do not deserve special rights! According to the United States Supreme Court, "any person seeking protective minority class status must satisfy three elements: immutable characteristics like race and gender, financial discrimination and political weakness." This group must be clearly identified by physical characteristics, such as skin color or gender, that defines them as an insular and discreet group.

Sodomites do not fit any of those descriptions! They have not been deprived of the basic rights that are available to all Americans. They certainly have not suffered economic discrimination, nor have they been denied the opportunity for an education, job, or social standard.

According minority status to homosexuals is a slap in the face of every racial minority in the United States. Once this devious attempt is legitimized, homosexuals will go after your children next. They are already promoting their life-style in the preschools and kindergartens of our nation without the knowledge of unsuspecting parents. Books like *Heather Has Two Mommies,* and *Daddy's Roommate* are being read today by first graders in our public school systems.

Martha Swift writes in the *Gay Community News,* "We shall sodomize your sons, emblems of your feeble masculinity. We shall seduce them in your schools, in your dormitories, in your gymnasiums and your locker rooms, in your sports arenas, in your seminaries and in your youth groups."[3] Homosexuals are well-organized, well-funded, and dead serious about proselytizing your children and mine. God help us if they ever win the battle for America's children!

Despite all of the positive media attention to homosexuals, the average American is still overwhelmingly antihomosexual. There is something about the very nature of homosexuality that runs contrary to the very nature of our humanity. It is contrary to the laws of nature and to the laws of God. One would have to rip out several sections of the Bible and throw them away in order to claim to be a Christian and take a pro-homosexual position.

Friends in high places

President Clinton has done almost everything possible within his power to promote the homosexual agenda. In a video presentation at the "Gay and Lesbian Ball" which was conducted on the evening of his presidential inauguration, he said: "I just want to thank the gay and lesbian community for their courage and commitment. I have a vision, and you're part of it."

The tragedy is that Mr. Clinton and his cronies haven't comprehended that as soon as homosexuals have their rights, the next group of sexual perverts will expect to have theirs as well! Pedophiles (who enjoy having sex with little children) are waiting in the wings to begin campaigning for their "rights." The "rights" to molest your children!

God also has a vision for unrepentant homosexuals. You will see them under the Dead Sea and under several layers of fire and brimstone! God certainly offers the opportunity of salvation and repentance to homosexuals, but to those who refuse to repent of their perverted sin, there is only a fearful expectation of judgment.

Despite the strong statements in the Bible against homosexuality, the Clinton-Gore administration has continued to court the homosexual and lesbian community. They have hosted numerous meetings, luncheons, and banquets with blatant homosexuals.

The highest suicide rate in America is among homosexuals. Why? Because it is unnatural and violates the human conscience. It also offends the nature of God and His laws. The pulpits of our nation must cry out against this wicked sin! If we fail to do so, we're going to forsake our children and bring the judgment of God upon our nation.

Jerry Falwell took a strong stand against the homosexual movement in the 1970s and received a great deal of abuse from the media for his position. I, for one, salute his courage in speaking out against this deadly sin. Dr. Falwell has observed: "History proves homosexuality reaches a pandemic level in societies in crisis or in a state of collapse."[4] Homosexuality is a difficult and complex problem that often results in deep emotional pain for those who feel trapped in it. Just because a person has a temptation in that regard does not mean that they have to surrender their behavior or their thought patterns to that temptation. Even as responsible heterosexuals must exercise self-control, so must those who are tempted toward homosexual sin. I believe they can truly change from within by the power and grace of God.

Homosexual activists, however, are given over to the propagation of the homosexual life-style. They are determined to do everything they can to prey upon the young people of America and recruit them into their life-style. The ultimate tragedy is that the liberal media that has encouraged this and promoted the acceptance of the homosexual life-style to the threat of the traditional American family.

For example, in 1989 the New York State Supreme Court ruled that a homosexual couple living together must be considered a "family" under the New York Rent Control Regulations. In 1990 the City of San Francisco adopted a "domestic partner" ordinance by referendum, permitting homosexual couples to register their relationship in the city as a legal partnership. *American Demographics* magazine has predicted that by the middle of the 21st Century, domestic relationships will be recognized in all major jurisdictions of the United States.[5] The Lotus Corporation, a computer software company, has already established a benefits package for "domestic partners" of company employees.

Homosexual myths

Two of the predominate myths promoted by the homosexual community are that homosexuality is genetically caused, and that it involves about 10% of the American population. Neither of these conclusions has been successfully documented. Psychologist Dr. Stanton Jones has observed that the concept of a homosexual orientation leading to a stable, lifelong pattern just cannot be proven from psychological or sociological evidence. He concludes: "It appears homosexuality can develop without genetic or hormonal factors, but generally does not develop without education and socialization."[6]

The myth that 10% of the population is a statistic generated by the Kinsey Report and cannot be taken seriously. Kinsey's basic data was gathered from criminals, including sex offenders, and then the results were applied to the general population. A study done by the National Opinion and Research Center in Chicago found that only 3% of the population claimed at least one homosexual act per year.

Another myth promoted by the homosexual community is the myth of safe sex. Condom usage is not even successful in the prevention of pregnancy, let alone the prevention of the spread of AIDS! The World Health Organization (WHO) estimates that as many as ten million people are already infected by the HIV virus. Currently, over 500,000 Americans are being diagnosed with AIDS each year. Further, the World Health Organization predicts that by the year 2,000, at least 30 million people will be infected with AIDS worldwide.[7]

It is generally assumed that AIDS began in Africa and spread rapidly by homosexual contact and then by heterosexual intercourse. In the United States it is estimated that about 60% of all AIDS cases can be attributed to homosexual activity, but it is only a matter of time until AIDS spreads throughout the promiscuous heterosexual community as well. The excessive extramarital activity in our society is dramatically increasing the number of sexually transmitted diseases, including AIDS.

The spread of syphilis, chlamydia, and genital herpes are at an all-time high in the American population. It is estimated that over 20 million Americans are infected with some form of serious sexually transmitted disease.[8]

Since 1970 the federal government has spent more than 2 billion dollars to promote "safe sex." During that period of time, the number of teenage pregnancies and sexually transmitted diseases among teenagers has more than quadrupled! During the same time our government has spent less than 8 million dollars promoting sexual abstinence. This amount, stretched over a period of 20 years, is almost insignificant.

The government has adopted the attitude that "everybody is doing it," so we might as well assume kids are going to have sex and encourage them to do all they can to "protect" themselves.

In his insightful book, *Before It's Too Late*, David Jeremiah lists the following advances that the gay rights community is making in our nation today:[9]

- Homosexual men and women are "coming out of the closet" as never before and galvanizing support from the liberal media.
- The Civil Service Commission has issued guidelines making it impossible for federal employment to be denied to homosexuals.
- 120 major national corporations including AT&T and IBM, have announced that they will not discriminate in the hiring of employees.

- The television programs, movies, and sitcoms constantly promote programming which involves homosexual characters, virtually always portrayed in a positive light.
- The Metropolitan Community Church, largely made up of homosexuals, headquartered in Los Angeles, has over 100 congregations and mission stations nationwide.
- Gay Rights legislation is continually being sought to elevate homosexuality to the status of a minority, giving it legitimacy and normalcy.
- The American Psychological Asso. (APA) no longer lists homosexuality as "abnormal" behavior in its *Diagnostical and Statistical Manual III.*

Is there any hope?

Homosexuality is being spread by the television and movie industry faster than any other method. The impact of the media has almost convinced an unsuspecting public that homosexuality is normal, acceptable and even desirable. If we are to have any hope of reversing this tragic situation, we must act now! Let me suggest several steps that are essential for the Christian community:

1. We must reject any attempt to reinterpret the Bible in light of the sinfulness of our culture.

Whenever a society falls into sin, it will almost always attempt to readjust its interpretation of scripture in order to justify that sin. We cannot capitulate to liberal theologians who are suggesting that the love of God is the only standard by which human behavior should be judged. While God certainly loves sinners of all types, He also is a God of holiness who judges unrepentant sin. We cannot continue to live in sin - any kind of sin - and shake our fist at heaven and expect to escape the judgment of God.

2. We must reject the idea that a Spirit-filled Christian can be a practicing homosexual at the same time.

The entire emphasis of scripture mitigates against this very idea! It is impossible to enter the kingdom of heaven while rejecting the standards of the King. One cannot maintain Christian integrity and condone any life-style which God condemns. This is just as true for adultery, incest, rape, and sexual abuse, as it is for homosexuality and lesbianism. We might just as well turn our churches over to adulterers, murderers and robbers! The church exists to call sinners out of their sins. Our God-given mandate is to redeem a fallen world to a Savior who can transform them from their sin. There is no place in the legitimate Christian church for an encouragement of any life-style that rejects a biblical definition of true and legitimate Christianity.

3. **We must refuse to allow our opponents to put us on the defensive.**

The homosexual community loves to criticize the evangelical Christian community for a lack of love or compassion, but it is not love and compassion to condone a sinful life-style that will ultimately lead to permanent personal destruction. Love is not telling someone what they want to hear, but what they need to hear! Genuine love does not condone sin, but confronts it for the ultimate good of the sinner.

4. **As good citizens we must do everything we can to support candidates who will defend the traditional family.**

It is impossible to give the militant homosexual community what it wants without condemning our young people by the millions to a lifetime of misery. This is too high a price to pay. I will speak out against any candidate who advocates the normalization of homosexuality and the destruction of the Christian family as long as I have breath in my body. I gave my two legs to defend this country from communism, and I would not hesitate to give every last ounce of my life and breath to defend it from immorality. We are facing a far greater enemy today which threatens to undermine our national stability from within. There can be no compromise with the homosexual agenda!

5. **We must reach out with genuine Christian love and compassion to those who are struggling to be free from the sin of homosexuality.**

Our concern about this particular sin no more condemns the sinner than our concern about any other sinful behavior. The

Bible reminds us: "For all have sinned and come short of the glory of God" (Romans 3:23).

The Scripture also reminds us that many of the early Christians were converted out of sinful heterosexual and homosexual life-styles. Writing to the church at Corinth, the Apostle Paul said, "And such were some of you: but ye are washed, but ye are sanctified, but ye are justified in the name of the Lord Jesus, and by the Spirit of our God." There is hope for the homosexual sinner just as there is hope for the heterosexual sinner. The same Savior's grace is available to one and all who will receive it. The call of Scripture is the same, irregardless of one's sin. If we are willing to confess our sins, repent of them, and receive Jesus Christ as the Lord and Savior of our lives, we can be set free from any sin of any kind.

If you are caught in the sin of homosexuality, please don't believe the lie of government, the media, and secular society. It will lead you down a road of destruction. It will weave a web of guilt and deception which will only increase your sense of bondage. Don't be afraid to acknowledge your sin, and turn to the Savior who alone can set you free. If you have struggled with what position to take on this issue as a believer, please let me urge you to examine what the Bible says about the sin of homosexuality for yourself. The opinions of those who want to nullify the seriousness of this sin are only contributing to the further demise of those who are caught in its unnatural web. There is freedom available to all who will receive it.

The Lord Jesus Himself said, "And ye shall know the truth and the truth shall make you free" (John 8:32). There is no real freedom apart from that spiritual liberation which God grants to those who will receive it from Him as a free gift of His grace. Our Lord does not call us unto Himself to entrap us into some kind of legalistic bondage or to take away the joy from our lives, rather, it is only in Him that we are truly set free from the destructive and addictive behaviors which are destined to ruin our lives. That is why Jesus said, "I am come that they might have life, and that they might have it more abundantly" (John 10:10). That abundant life is available to all who will repent of their sin and return to the Savior and be truly set free!

"Children learn their basic
concepts of security,
interdependence and respect
for authority from observing
the relationship of a wife
and husband."

—Jerry Falwell
Chancellor, Liberty University

Chapter 7

Family Values
Reawakening the American Dream

The role of a happy and stable family is one that underlies the American hope for a better future. A nation is no stronger than the families who make it up, and our nation has benefited over the years from strong family ties. But those family bonds are being shattered today at a rapid rate, and many have given up hope on the future of the family. Consider these statistics:

- In 1970, 11% of all American children lived in single-parent homes: By 1990 that percentage had risen to 20%.

- Despite the efforts of some excellent single parents, the National Center for Health Statistics reports that children from single-parent homes are 100 times more likely to suffer emotional problems and physical abuse. Single-parent children are twice as likely to drop out of high school.

- Every year, over 1 million American children watch

87

their parents divorce. Kids feel fear, abandonment, and loneliness. These effects do not fade quickly; in fact, studies done on the effects of divorce on the adult children of divorce show that the consequences of divorce last for a lifetime.[1]

- Another study concluded that the "most reliable predictor of crime is neither poverty nor race, but growing up fatherless."[2]

- Father absence, including the disappearance of some fathers, has become a national epidemic. 87% of all children of divorce still end up with their mothers.

The revolt against the family

Jerry Falwell has said:

The American family is in a revolution. It is not a revolution with guns, insurrections, and rioting in the streets...This revolution is fought with words, ideas, insinuations, and clashes over values. It is a revolution that permeates schools, legislative bodies, television shows, politics, our courts, businesses, and even our places of worship...It is a revolution which will determine the fate and the future of the traditional American family.[3]

Christians are not the only ones concerned about the future of the family. *Fortune* magazine recently stated:

The revolution in families that we see all around us — the result of an epidemic of divorce, remarriage, redivorce, illegitimacy and — within intact families— has precipitated a revolution in the inner lives of our children. In a torrent of recent research —that this revolution with the minds and hearts of the next generation has deeply troubling implications for the American social order.[4]

Newsweek also echoes a similar alarm:

The numbers are daunting. There is a high correlation between disrupted homes and just about every social problem in America today. According to research, more than 80% of the adolescents in psychiatric hospitals come from broken families.[5]

Any statistical evaluation of the problems facing the family are further complicated by the fact that living together has become socially acceptable. Abortion is legal, and remaining single and childless is now commonplace.

Over the past three decades family life in America has changed so dramatically that it is as if it has gone through the effects of a social and political revolution. Hundreds of thousands of men, women, and children are being victimized by the selfishness of parents who chose their own self-interest over the personal concerns of their children. I have never been able to comprehend how a mother or father could simply walk away from their own children to satisfy their own lusts. Yet, this happens hundreds of thousands of times every year! Today's family is far from what it once was, yet the traditional family is not dead, and neither is it dying! It is still true that 79% of all families involve people who are living together, who are related by blood, marriage, or adoption, and headed by a married couple.

The crisis is in the other 29%. Instead of moving away from the traditional family, new evidence points to the fact that there is a trend back toward stable family living. Those who were raised in broken homes realize the need for stable families, and those who were raised in traditional families clearly understand the benefit of their family experience. The real crisis is in what has been called the "sexual revolution." The impact of changing mores in American behavior has virtually destroyed about 1/4 of the American adult population. As teenagers some of them bought the "new morality," and they have spent the last twenty to thirty years paying for it! Tragically, some of the social policy-makers in our government have attempted to justify, rather than rectify this problem. They have advocated more social welfare in order to deal with the children of single-parent families, while doing little or nothing to save marriages and prevent divorce.

Dr. Falwell, Chancellor of Liberty University, has stated: We have seen an entire generation of misguided young people grow up to become a generation of misinformed and out-of-control parents."[6] According to Everett Ladd of the Raper Center for Public Opinion and Research, most Americans have experienced considerable anxiety about losing their family values. People are concerned about crime in the streets, terrorizing the neighborhoods, and the continued decline in the quality of public education. All of these point to a widespread uneasiness about the state of the nation's morals and the stability of its families.

A biblical definition of the family

According to the Bible, God decreed the existence of the family, the church, and government. As such, the family is a God-ordained institution founded upon the marriage of a man and a woman, promising to remain faithful to one another as husband and wife for an entire lifetime. This biblical definition of a family is what has been traditionally called a "nuclear" family. Add the grandparents, aunts, uncles, cousins, and other relatives, and you have what has generally been called the "expanded" family.

This definition is the biblical ideal. It is not intended to rule out the legitimacy of "single-parent" families or "blended" families. The Bible itself is certainly full of such examples (eg. Judah, Joseph, and David).

In their recent book, *Children at Risk*, James Dobson and Gary Bauer provide a definition of traditional families that is both biblical and inclusive of families that include single-parent families, blended families, and families with no children in the home.

They provide the following definition of a traditional family:

1. A man and woman committed to a lifelong marriage.
2. Commitment to bearing and raising children to the glory of God.
3. Family members who are related by marriage, birth, or adoption.
4. The inherent worth of each individual in the family, regardless of his or her productivity.

5. Basic values which include fidelity, loyalty, self-discipline, commitment and chastity.[7]

The proper understanding of the family is to understand who we are, where we fit, and why we exist. The security of the family provides the atmosphere in which psychologically and spiritually healthy individuals may be raised to make a valuable contribution to society. Edith Schaeffer says the faith of the family is a "formation center for human relationships."[8] The family is the place where you learn to understand that we are significant, worthwhile, and have meaning and purpose in this world. Ideally, the Christian family is the place where children learn that God loves them and has a great purpose for their lives.

The family is the preliminary place for developing a child's awareness of God. It is in the loving environment of the Christian home that children experience relationships which spiritually encourage and sustain their walk with God. It is in the home that children learn who God is, why we need Him, and how much He loves us. The tragedy today is that these basic family values are being undermined in our public schools, courtrooms, workplaces, movie studios, and even in the halls of Congress!

There is no doubt that a great cultural war is underway in our society. This was certainly underscored when former Vice President Dan Quayle gave a speech about the importance of family values and family commitments. In that speech he made reference to the fictional TV character Murphy Brown, as being an example that contradicts the very values for which he was speaking. He immediately became the brunt of critical editorials, public jokes, and an excessive smear campaign by the media. Nevertheless, after the speech, every opinion poll showed everyone in agreement with the vice president. A *Houston Post* call-in poll gave the vice president a margin of 10,387 in favor, and 1,866 against. That is a margin of nearly 85%!

In his now famous speech, Quayle said:

Right now, the failure of our families is hurting America deeply. When families fall, society falls. Children need love and discipline. They need mothers and fathers. A welfare check is not a husband. The state is not a father. It is from parents that children come to understand values and themselves as men and women, mothers and fathers...

It doesn't help matters when prime-time TV has Murphy Brown — a character who supposedly epitomizes today's intelligent, highly paid, professional women — mocking the importance of a father by bearing a child alone, and calling it just another "life-style choice"...

So I think the time has come to renew our public commitment to our Judeo-Christian values — in our churches, in our synagogues, in our civic organizations and our schools. We are, as our children recite each morning, "one nation under God." That's a useful reminder for acknowledging a deity and an authority higher than our own pleasure and personal ambitions.[9]

Family values, like all basic values, are based in biblical truth. These values do not merely arise out of some vague sense of corporate opinion, but from the inspired Word of God.

These values are the essential basis for a Christian understanding of marriage and family, parents and children, fathers and mothers. Those who decry the imposition of Christian values in society are just as quick to advocate non-Christian values as the model for our society and its families.

This is not an issue of imposing Christian beliefs upon a non-Christian society. Rather, it is the very opposite! It is the imposition of non-Christian values on a predominantly Christian society. It does not mean that the vast majority of the American public is necessarily made up of born-again believers, yet we are still a nation who has a common heritage in the Christian family of our national principles. Those principles are at the very core and foundation of what American family values are all about. If they are ever removed, the vacuum that is left will be so enormous that America, as we know it, will fall into the pit of moral and social oblivion!

The war against the family
During the past two decades, the liberal element of our

society has declared all-out war on the family. The welfare system has promoted a welfare mentality that quickly becomes anti-family. As long as our government is willing to fund unwed pregnancies, we will only continue to encourage welfare mothers to continue to produce children outside the bond of marriage. As long as our government continues to promote the legalization of abortion, we will never see our nation return to moral values on any issues related to marriage and family living.

If our government spent as much time trying to improve conditions for traditional American families as they spend promoting nontraditional values, our society would be much better for it.

Instead, we find our own tax money going to support the very institutions which are decidedly antifamily. Planned Parenthood is the most politically powerful and financially supported antifamily institution in America today. Organized by Margaret Sanger, an advocate of sexual freedom, Planned Parenthood was initially granted government support on the grounds it would help reduce illegitimate pregnancies. To the contrary, illegitimate pregnancy is at an all-time high despite the efforts of Planned Parenthood's hype and promotion of condoms distribution in public schools and their complete and total support for abortion on demand.

The National Organization for Women (NOW) has 250,000 registered members. At the heart of their agenda is a liberal feminist philosophy which goes out of its way to promote lesbianism, adultery, and sexual permissiveness. By contrast, Beverly LaHaye's Concerned Women for America (CWA) has a membership of more than 600,000 women. But you will rarely hear from them in the media because the vast majority of women who are in the forefront of our public media are sympathetic to the position and agenda of the NOW.

By contrast, CWA is often avoided by the media on the excuse that "we already know what they're going to say." It is high time that Christians in America stood up and demanded equal time! Every pastor in America ought to be defending the CWA from his pulpit on a regular basis. There is not a finer organization of concerned Christian women anywhere in the world. They have fought against every possible prejudice in the media, and every kind of legislative proposal that is against the traditional American family. For men in the pulpits of this nation to stand up and say nothing about this is the height of hypocrisy. Beverly LaHaye and her associates are to be congratulated, encouraged, and commended for their efforts.

The National Abortion Rights Action League (NARAL) is another antifamily organization. It is the militant arm of the pro-abortion movement. A sister organization of NOW, it supports the liberal, antifamily movement.

Probably the most powerful of all anti-health and family organizations is the American Civil Liberties Union (ACLU). Randall Terry, former head of Operation Rescue, has observed: "The ACLU is the world's oldest, largest, most influential association of lawyers, political activists, and social reformers."[10]

Rebecca Hagelin recently stated in a column in *USA Today*:

Public acknowledgment of God's existence is part of our culture and heritage. Banning God from public life is the rod on which the ACLU intends to hang its own version of the Iron Curtain across America.[11]

Our secular media!

The real problem in America today is the anti-God hatred that predominates so many areas of our American society. While it does not represent the sentiments of a vast majority of Americans, unfortunately it does represent the outspoken opinion of many secularists whose voices are being carried by our public media to every hamlet and corner of this nation. While we acknowledge their freedom of speech and right to their own opinions, we cannot and must not sit back and say or do nothing about it. As believers, we too have every right to express our beliefs and opinions, without government interference or reprisal. This certainly includes freedom from the interference of the media itself who so often castigate Christian believers as fanatics, extremists, and even dangerous elements of our society. There is nothing more dangerous than the bias and prejudice within our secular media! We are not calling for the cancellation of anyone else's freedom of speech, but we are asking for a fair hearing from the public media. It matters little if one has the right to hold his own personal opinions, if those opinions are constantly berated from the public press, newscasts, and the entertainment segment.

The American public is amusing itself to death, while the mass media reshapes our values, political and religious beliefs, and our personal behavior by getting us to laugh at the very things that are destroying the family in America today. Jerry Falwell has observed: "90 million Americans watch television every night, and its one-way message has a profound influence on the national character."[12]

The impact of television alone is startling! A typical 14-year-old boy watches three hours of television daily and does just one hour of homework. By the time a child finishes elementary school, he or she has witnessed 100,000 acts of violence and 8,000 murders. Each year the major television networks depict over 10,000 acts of sexual indecency...93% of them outside of marriage.

The aftermath of the war: Empty lives

The real problem is that the demise of family values in our culture has resulted in the devastation of the traditional American family. When we understand that in personalized terms, we begin to realize its terrible impact on broken marriages, desperate women, and struggling children — all of whom feel the harmful effects of the war against the family. Tragically, our public media continues to glorify the image of free sex, promiscuous living, and the general irresponsibility toward life and family.

These shifting values have left millions of Americans confused about who they are, what they believe, and where they are going. The "values revolution" that is going on in our nation today is taking its toll on each succeeding generation. With millions of young people growing up as the adult children of divorce (ACD), millions of Americans are hurting, longing and empty inside. They have no real guidelines for maintaining marriage, raising children, or building a family for the glory of God. Left to their own devices, they are living their lives simply for themselves, and their spouses and children are the ones who are suffering the consequences.

A general atmosphere of meaninglessness pervades the American scene today. In that empty, anxious, rootlessness which is a common experience for so many people, we find every kind of emotional anxiety and conflict imaginable. Child abuse is at an all-time high. Marital infidelity is out of control. Sexual promiscuity is rampant. Guilt, loneliness, and anxiety have quieted the American conscience. You cannot live in sin without suffering sin's consequences.

Whenever we preach on the moral consequences of sinful living, and define the issues of right and wrong on the standards of scripture, there will always be an outcry from those who are living in the dirty clutches of sinful immorality; but we must not stop preaching against that sin while clearly announcing God's love and grace and forgiveness to the sinner. No preacher of the gospel enjoys announcing the sins of others. Certainly, no true gospel preacher believes he is immune to the temptation of sin himself, but you cry out first of all because we love God and His truth! We cannot be silent and watch a generation destroy itself. We cry out because we genuinely love people, despite the fact that they are destroying themselves. To fail to speak up would be a contradiction of our love and concern for those who will certainly suffer the consequences of their own sinful and irresponsible actions.

In order to resolve the family values conflicts which we see today, we must pledge ourselves to do everything we can to preserve the heritage of the family in America. I believe that we have a God-given mandate to do so. We cannot allow the anti-family segment of our society to destroy this nation which has been so blessed of God. If they want to destroy their own families, that is their own business; but we cannot let them destroy our families in the process, nor can we allow them to destroy the sacredness of the concept of the family as a God-given institution in our society. No other arrangement has ever been successful. The family worked because God is the author of the family, and the sustainer of it. Until we are willing to build our families on the principles of the Word of God, practical Godly living, and genuine Christian love, there will be little hope for the future.

I am not a pessimist, nor am I an idealist: I am a realist! I realize the family is in trouble today in our secular society, but I also realize that some of the greatest families our nation has ever known are flourishing today in Christian homes and churches across this nation. We have an opportunity, by building strong families to the glory of God, to show the world there is a better way to do it. Secularism may attempt to destroy the traditional family, but it will offer nothing of lasting significance in its place. The Christian home will ultimately stand supreme in a decadent society as the only lasting social unit that is worth our time and effort. With families falling all around us, we must be more committed than ever to our marriages, our children and our families. As these families stand the test of time, they will in and of themselves become a growing testimony to the truth of the Scripture and the power of God. In each home we must do everything we can to promote the traditional American family, to support those political candidates who will empower such families, and oppose those candidates whose proposed legislation would undermine the traditional family.

In some cases this will mean voting out of office those who oppose the traditional American family. It will mean supporting candidates who support the family. It will mean supporting candidates who will appoint the kind of judges to the highest level of courts in our land who will also support and defend traditional family values, and in some cases, it will mean sacrificially supporting those ministries and organizations who are determined to support and encourage Judeo-Christian values and the traditional family, which is the hope of America's future.

"The hard truth is that while man may say he wants to do the right thing, more often than not he has self-interest in mind. He uses his intellect to build an acceptable theology for the passions and practices of his life."

— Pastor David Jeremiah,
Shadow Mountain
Community Church
El Cajon, California

Chapter 8

Lack of Medical Ethics
Reinventing the Future

When Aldous Huxley wrote *Brave New World* in 1932, he foresaw the future in the form that is now taking shape today. Instead of the Big Brother of George Orwell's *1984*, Huxley foresaw a world gone mad in materialism and pleasure seeking to deaden its conscience against the emptiness of high technology. His vision of the future included human fertilization "farms," artificial insemination and genetic selection.

Huxley pictured the future as the mindless pursuit of one's existence, controlled by machines and soothed by the endless pursuit of pleasure. The past would become meaningless. Noble pursuits would give way to the all-consuming pursuit of pleasure. The world of the future, which Huxley foresaw, was one that would readily sacrifice its principles for pleasure. It was a world unified politically and economically, whose God was itself — the World State.

Such predictions seemed incredible and unbelievable at the time, but now, just a generation later, the unimaginable has become reality. We are living in a time when technology is being developed faster than our society is able to slow down and ask relevant moral questions about its use in our lives. With the Christian base of morality eroded from the general culture, it is little wonder that our intellectual leaders are incapable of formulating a proper understanding of the use of modern miracle technology and its moral and social implications in our daily lives. Abortion, euthanasia, assisted suicides, genetic engineering, and fetal tissue transplants are all a part of the real medical world of our time.

U.S. Senator Jesse Helms has said:

> There comes a time in the history of all great civilizations when the moral foundations upon which it rests are shaken by some momentous turn of events. That time has come for America. Great nations die when they cease to exist by great principles which give them a vision and strength to rise above tyranny and human degradation.[1]

Former United States Surgeon General, C. Everett Koop, has stated:

> We are a schizophrenic society. We will fly a deformed newborn baby 400 miles by airplane to perform a series of remarkable operations on such a youngster, knowing full well that the end result will be far less than perfect. We will ship food to a starving nation overseas, and at the same time supply arms to its enemy. We will stop a cholera epidemic by vaccine in a country unable to feed itself, so that the people can survive cholera in order to die of starvation. While we struggle to save the life of a preterm baby in a hospital's newborn intensive care unit, obstetricians in that same hospital are destroying similar infants yet unborn.[2]

It should not surprise us that our nation is faced with such incredible moral dilemmas. The new morality situation ethics have mitigated against the absolute standards of the Word of God. According to Joseph Fletcher, the founder of modern situation ethics, all laws, codes and rules are outmoded, obsolete and no longer binding on human kind. The only authoritative law is "the law of love." Fletcher states:

> Anything and everything is right or wrong according to the situation, and the goal is to find absolute love's relative course.[3]

David Jeremiah, pastor of Shadow Mountain Community Church in El Cajon, California, and speaker on Turning Point Radio Broadcast, states:

> The new morality is a revolt against the principles and guidelines of God's Word. It is a permissiveness that says, 'If no one is hurt, anything goes.' It is built upon humanistic philosophy that believes man is basically good, and given the right education, job, and environment, he will make right and loving choices.[4]

The death of truth

The advocates of the new morality emphasize that love is the only real absolute. All other absolutes based upon concepts of truth are eradicated or eliminated. The basic philosophy of Fletcher's new morality is that: (1) Love is the only norm; (2) Love and justice are the same; (3) Love justifies its means. The popular acceptance of this kind of thinking leads to the idea that one can redefine that which is true or right or proper based on one's definition of love. Love becomes a very subjective condition based upon the given situation of the moment. In an attempt to justify his position, Fletcher tells the story of the rainmaker from the play by Richard Nash. The rainmaker made his living by convincing the ranchers he could bring rain in the midst of a drought. While at a particular ranch, the rainmaker feels sorry for the rancher's daughter who is a lonely and rejected individual. In order to restore the girl's sense of womanliness, he commits sexual fornication with her. The girl's brother finds out and threatens to shoot the rainmaker. However, the girl's wise old rancher father grabs the gun away from him and says, "Noah, you're so full of what's right, you can't see what's good."

According to this concept, love is to be understood in terms of good intentions and well-intended consequences. In other words, the end justifies the means! If the Bible had followed this line of thinking, Joseph would have jumped in bed with Potiphar's wife, instead of refusing her advances!

What's wrong with this kind of thinking! It has captured the popular appeal in most of our secular institutions, because it uses the idea of love as an excuse for misbehavior.

1. It separates love from truth.

There can be no real love unless it rests upon a concept of truth. In the new morality, each moral decision is measured by the subjective feelings of the individual. In reality, the individual, not God, becomes the basis of all human authority in ethical decisions.

Theologian Carl Henry has observed:

> When the individual is left wholly to himself to decide what legitimate forms his love for his neighbor might take, he soon and often becomes a tyrant toward his neighbor, the victim. When love has not been codified in bonding love, the lover himself becomes the law... If the new morality were readily adopted, civil law would lose its moral basis to bring any man to trial for his deeds. If no conceivable human action is per se immoral and sinful, if there is no prescriptive ethics, if no one but the person himself can decide in his own situation if any act is right or wrong, there is no moral basis for prosecuting any man at law for any act he might commit.[5]

2. It places man above God.

The situation advocated by modern ethicists is not unlike that of the one that existed in the Book of Judges. The Scriptures state over and over that there was no king in Israel and "every man did that which was right in his own eyes" (Judges 21:25). Notice that everyone was doing what he believed to be right on the basis of his own definition.

The tragedy is that the Book of Judges is filled with horrible ethical violations: adultery, sexual abuse, rape, murder, idolatry and genocide. One has only to read the closing chapters of the book (17-21) to realize that so-called "situation ethics" ends in moral and civil catastrophe.

Whenever morality is reduced to personal preference there is no basis for moral thinking. The great problem with all humanistic philosophies of life is that they make man the center of all things — instead of God. As a result, the unbeliever ends up viewing the world inside out and upside down. He sees it from a self-centered perspective, instead of viewing the world from a God-centered perspective.

3. It covers a "hidden agenda."

David Jeremiah remarks: "The hard truth is that while man may say he wants to do the right thing, more often than not he has self-interest in mind. He uses his intellect to build an acceptable theology for the passions and practices of his life."[6] It does not matter how much you try to mask over your sin with intellectual rationalization, sin is still sin, and the church of the living God must rise up and call it what it really is! We have come to a time when it is no longer popular or even acceptable to denounce sin as sin. We have a generation of people who would rather have their ears "tickled" than face the hard fact of life. But the truth is, we are facing the most serious moral and ethical crises of our time, and this is no time to mince words. We must address the ethical issues that challenge our beliefs and find the answers and the direction that this generation so desperately needs.

Genetic Engineering

It is now possible that scientific technology will reach the state where human beings can be completely and totally "repackaged." Heart and liver transplants are now commonplace, and it is only a matter of time when other major organ transplants will be possible as well. Micro-surgery enables doctors to operate on specific parts of the human brain that control specific functions such as seeing, thinking, hearing, etc. It will only be a matter of time until they will have the technical ability to reprogram the human mind. These possibilities have potentially frightening consequences for future generations.

Professor Sir Norman Anderson of the University of London has warned:

If the use of human beings to test out the efficacy — and the possibility of dangerous side effects - of new drugs is regarded by the medical profession as irresponsible unless done in accordance with strictly defined criteria; then how much more must even the most avant-garde research worker quail before the terrifying possibilities inherent in any tinkering with the genetic future of the human race, or of its individual members.[7]

If our society was still grounded in its Christian heritage, we might have some reason for hope that the medical community would make the kind of decisions in regard to biomedical ethics that would bring honor and glory to God. But that time has long since passed. We can only imagine that secular voices will attempt to prevail in the current debate and push the frontiers of biomedical research further and further to the limits.

I am not a medical doctor, nor do I propose to have all the solutions to fit every medical dilemma our society may be facing in the area of medical technology; but I am gravely concerned when the medical community seems to want to bulldoze ahead with little or no regard to the sanctity and decency of human life. When babies can be aborted just for the sake of convenience and the excuse that their body tissue is necessary for medical research, I have to drop my head in shame, and sit in disbelief and ask, "But what if that were your life that was being taken for a convenience and the expediency of someone else?" There is a great difference between giving up your life willingly, and that of having it taken from you deliberately and maliciously.

When I went to Vietnam, I realized that I was putting my life in jeopardy for the sake of defending the nation I love. There is a great deal of difference between that kind of commitment and a murderer breaking into my home, uninvited, and attempting to take my life. This is exactly the type of problem we have in the field of medical ethics today.

Sir Norman Anderson goes on to remark:

Nor is the Christian exempt from any of these dangers. He should, indeed, be more conscious than the human- ists that man is both finite and sinful; and this should serve as a continual reminder of the catastrophic mistakes he can make, even with the most laudable intentions, and a perpetual warning against that arrogance of spirit which forgets the obedient and dependence which the creature always owes to the Creator.[8]

Artificial insemination

We first began to hear of the issue of genetic engineering in relation to artificial insemination. The semen and egg from a man and woman could be frozen in liquid nitrogen and artificially joined in a glass dish (in vitro). For the first time in human history, it was possible for the scientists to become breeding experts. The issue of genetic selection and manipulation became a reality during the twentieth century. Children could be artificially inseminated and surgically placed in a woman's womb who had not gotten pregnant through conventional means. She could then carry the baby to full term and deliver the child. Then questions began to be raised about surrogate mothers who would "rent" their wombs for the production of healthy babies which other women were incapable of bearing. The argument was raised that this would provide healthy children for couples who were infertile and were unable to get pregnant and have children of their own.

Then the issue of the artificial insemination donor came to the surface. Men were donating semen to "sperm banks" where it could be used later in the fertilization of a female egg. This meant that a person could "father" a child by a woman they had never met, and a person with whom they had never had any kind of relationship, social or otherwise. Then the issue was raised as to whose property these fertilized eggs were. Couples in the midst of donating sperm and eggs might end up in a divorce proceeding and argue that they did not want to bring the child to birth that they had artificially inseminated with one another's reproductive elements. This eventually led to some sensational court battles in which the state, not God's Word, not the couples themselves, but the state decided who had the right to "own" these fertilized human beings.

Next we began reading about "fetal tissue transplants" from the physical elements of aborted fetuses. Initially many assumed that these so-called fetal transplants were being made from babies that were already considered "dead," but that is not the case! Fetal tissue transplants are actually taken from live fetuses (babies) and the very taking of the tissue brings about the baby's death. In other words, our government has authorized the slaughter or genocide of a generation of the unborn in order to make life more comfortable for those already among the living. In other words, we have succumbed to the idea that we have the right to guarantee the pursuit of happiness to one person at the expense of the right to life of another.

Euthanasia

Euthanasia is the medical term for the elimination of the elderly or the undesirable. Some have referred to it as "mercy killing." We have all read or heard about the accounts of Dr. Kervorkian, the so-called "Doctor Death" in Michigan, who willingly encourages doctor-assisted suicide for terminally ill patients. Despite the legal actions brought against him, Dr. Kervorkian has continued his deadly practice.

The rationale that is usually given for euthanasia is that we are simply helping people out of their misery. "You wouldn't want grandma to suffer any more, would you?" is the argument often raised. The problem is that euthanasia doesn't stop there: It eventually leads to the determination that anyone whose "quality of life" is questionable should be eliminated for their own good and for the general good of society. It is only a matter of time until this leads to the elimination of individuals whose ideas are contrary to that of the general society, and the elimination of these people will be looked upon as "good" for society in general.

Joni Eareckson Tada wrestles with this very issue in her book, *When Is It Right to Die?* Joni, herself a quadriplegic, a victim of a diving accident, looks back over the experience of her permanent paralysis, the death from cancer of her five-year-old niece, and the eventual death of her elderly father whose life ebbed away for weeks at the time in the hospital, and she reminds us that issues of medical ethics are not merely issues of philosophical debate, but flesh and blood and real people.

Joni comments:

Somewhere between those family tragedies, my thinking shifted, and I was forced to face an issue I had too long ignored. Ethics was no longer confined to the classroom. Standards of moral judgment now had flesh and blood, life and death reality...Twenty-five years in a wheelchair introduced me to the world of advocacy, and with it thousands of disabled people who were either sinking into or surfacing out of suicidal despair...During my years as a national disability advocate, I quickly saw how politicized these questions were becoming...Behind every newspaper story, every initiative on the ballot, every booklet printed by either a "right-to-die" or "right-to-life" group, was a family: a family like mine, a disabled person like me, a person, a family for whom my heart bled.[9]

All of us have read the difficult accounts of the families of Karen Quinlan and Nancy Cruzan, both of whom lay in a semicomatose state for years. The right-to-die question is a difficult one. Is it right to die when pain becomes more than one can bear, or if the medical costs reach a level where they are prohibitive, or where one's personal dignity is shattered? Where do we draw the line? Joni notes that euthanasia "conjures up images of everything from pulling the plug on a dying loved one to the killing of millions in Nazi Germany who were considered socially unuseful. Practically speaking, euthanasia means to produce death or assist an individual in achieving death because others, or even the patient himself, considers life no longer worth living."[10]

A real quality of life

Today the hot term is "quality of life." Medical technology has advanced to the stage where people's lives can be extended far beyond that which was ever thought possible in previous generations. Kidney machines, heart pacemakers, insulin injectors, and a host of other machines can increase the length of one's life. However, the ability to function does not necessarily insure a high degree of quality of life. Therefore, it is only a matter of time until society will ascribe to the physically fit and intellectually capable people a higher quality of life than those who have physical, mental, or social disabilities.

Once you legalize the elimination of people — for whatever reason — it is only a matter of time until a society eliminates anyone and everyone considered undesirable. Hitler proved that in Germany! Stalin proved it in Russia! Two African tribes proved that in Rwanda, and the Serbs are proving it in Bosnia! Whether we shoot them with a bullet, blow them away with a bomb, or simply eliminate them with a painless lethal injection — the end result is still the same! We, as Christians, cannot sit back and assume that a secularistic, humanistic, unbelieving society will eventually decide to do the right thing. In fact, there is no reason to even hope for such a solution! We must take action now to let our voice be heard on these crucial issues before they set in cement the moral values of the next generation. If we do not stand up for the rights of the unborn, the elderly, the infirm, the mentally retarded, those in wheelchairs, like myself, those who have been injured or wounded, it will only be a matter of time until someone begins calling for the elimination of Christians because they are a threat to the religious unity and compatibility of society.

Don't think it can't happen! Read the Book of Revelation. When the Antichrist comes to power and brings about a one-world government, one-world society, and one-world religion — it will be to the exclusion of all who oppose him. Biblical prophecy is filled with references to the "martyrs" who will be executed because of their testimony to Jesus Christ and their refusal to capitulate to the social unification of the new world order of the future.

We must make it clear that the doctors in this nation are not God! While they may have God-given gifts and opportunities to save and extend life, they are not the arbiters of who should live and who should die. If we do not insist that these issues be resolved by the absolute standards of the Word of God, and that God is sovereign over human life, we will be in danger of turning away from the ultimate quality of life which God Himself provides — and that is spiritual life which is eternal life.

"Although Hollywood is making more family-friendly products, parents must still exercise a deep level of discernment. Too many Christian moms and dads are blissfully unaware of the impact movies and television programs have on their children. Some parents have not taken steps to shield their children's eyes from those things involving sex and violence."

— Ted Baehr, Chairman of the Christian Film and Television Commission

Chapter 9

Media Perversion
Hollywood's War on Traditional Values

America is sick, and Hollywood is to blame. Not Hollywood as a place on a map, but the entertainment industry which has captured the heart and soul of this nation over the past 50 years. Dominated by unbelievers and people whose own lifestyles are openly immoral and anti-God, the entertainment industry has become the enemy of the traditional family.

Michael Medved, a well-known Hollywood film critic, and co-host of Sneak Previews, has said:

> America's long-running romance with Hollywood is over. As a nation we no longer believe that popular culture enriches our lives. Few of us view the show business capital as a magical source of uplifting entertainment, romantic inspiration, or even harmless fun. Instead, millions of Americans now see the entertainment industry as an all-powerful enemy, an alien force that assaults our most cherished values and corrupts our

children. The dream factory has become the poison factory.[1]

Despite our nation's concern for traditional family values, the entertainment industry has turned a deaf ear to our pleas. A 1989 Associate Press poll revealed that 80% of all Americans felt that movies contained too much profanity, and 82% objected that they contained too much violence. A 1990 *Parents* magazine poll revealed that 72% of their readers supported strict prohibition against "ridiculing or making fun of religion," and 64% supported restrictions on "ridiculing or making fun of traditional values, such as marriage and motherhood."

A Gallup Poll in 1991 revealed that 58% of Americans say that they are "offended frequently or occasionally" by prime-time television programming, and a recent Time/CNN survey showed the 67% of Americans believe that violent images in movies are to blame for the national epidemic of teenage violence.

Los Angeles Times columnist Cal Thomas announced at the end of 1990 that he was going to give up watching network television altogether. "They not only have abandoned my values," he wrote, "they now have sunk to the sewer level, dispensing the foulest of smells that resemble the garbage I take to the curb twice a week."[2]

The ravaging of our conscience

America no longer has a serious conscience about issues of right and wrong, sin and evil. Our moral conscience has been ravaged by the impact of the entertainment industry so long that we hardly believe anything anymore in America.

Tim and Beverly LaHaye have raised this same concern in their powerful book, *A Nation without Conscience*. In it, they observe that the entertainment artists have become the conscience of America. They observe that the combined impact of movies, television, theaters, and video bombards the minds of most of America's 250 million citizens...including many Christians who have lowered their personal standards. The LaHayes acknowledge:

Having been in church work all our lives, we find it

painful to admit that the men and women in the entertainment industry have more influence on the conscience of our nation than the preachers, parents, teachers, or anyone else. In fact, it is a very small group of individuals who hold our nation's morals hostage.[3]

Richard Neville has observed:

In my local video store, I see teenagers stockpiling at least ten hours of horror, porn, and pain for the weekend...As surely as toxic residue kills the fish and the fowl, so does sloth of our mean-spirited filmmakers and writers kill our spirit.[4]

Morality in Media tells us: "By the time the average child graduates from elementary school, he or she will have witnessed at least 8,000 murders and more than 100,000 other assorted acts of violence on television. Depending on the amount of time the child watches television, some youngsters could see more than 200,000 violent acts before they hit the streets of our nations as teenagers."[5]

Tom Elliff writes:

America's entertainment and media industry must bear much of the responsibility for much of our nation's precipitous moral decline over the past thirty years. It has ceased reflecting the moral values on which this nation was built, abusing its influence by engaging in a genuine veiled agenda of moral liberality.[6]

Against this trend stands the biblical injunction to "have no fellowship with the unfruitful work of darkness, but rather reprove them" (Eph. 5:11). It is time that the preachers of the gospel raised a strong word of warning against the evils that are being perpetuated by the movie and entertainment industry. It is time that we said, "Enough is enough!"

Taking a stand on entertainment

Ted Baehr, Chairman of the Christian Film and Television

Commission, has stated:

> Although Hollywood is making more family-friendly products, parents must still exercise a deep level of discernment. Too many Christian moms and dads are blissfully unaware of the impact movies and television programs have on their children. Some parents have not taken steps to shield their children's eyes from those things involving sex and violence.[7]

The Teenage Research Institute claims that teenagers watch an average of 50 movies a year in theaters, of which 80% are rated PG-13 or R! These same teenagers view another 50 movies a year on video at home or at the home of a friend. One of the problems our young people are struggling with today is a lack of discernment by parents. Baehr admits: "Christian families watch movies just as much as unchurched families."[8]

I believe it is time for the Christian community to take a stronger stand on the whole issue of the impact of pornography on television and in our movies. If that is the case, it is virtually impossible for Bible-believing Christians to support the movie industry as it is today. The more tolerant Christians have become of this industry, the less discerning they have become, and that lack of discernment is taking its toll on our children and their morals! Let me suggest these final steps for dealing with these issues in one's own heart:

- **Examine what you are watching**

  Too many parents lack discernment about their own viewing habits, and the viewing habits of their children. This is ultimately hypocritical. You cannot take your children to church and tell them you want God's best for them, while allowing them to be exposed to the worst possible video material available.

  I believe it is necessary for every parent to follow biblical guidelines for television viewing and any other involvement with the entertainment media. Make a list of the standards that you believe and determine not to allow material into your home which contradicts those standards. Make a list of the questionable things being said and done on various television programs, and match that with your list. It does not take a rocket scientist to discern that about 90% of that which you call "entertainment" violates basic biblical principles of morality.

- **Stand against evil**

The Scripture not only urges us to avoid evil, but to expose it. Sure, we can simply turn off our television sets. Or we can abstain from going to the movies. However, this alone does not solve the problem. The impact of the entertainment media has a stronger hold on American society. When the moral environment of our communities decline, it affects the moral values of our families as well, because we're part of that community.

Standing against evil is every believer's business! If necessary you may have to go to the manager of the convenience store and object to the content of various magazines and materials they sell in that store. Asking questions such as, "Do you know what's in this magazine?" can be very effective. Or questions like, "Would you want your children to see this?" You need to be willing to write letters of protest to the movie industry whether you have personally viewed the movie or not. Printed reviews of the movies are readily available in newspapers and can even be ordered from various Christian organizations. Here is a list of the major motion picture companies in this country.

Disney (Walt) Pictures/Hollywood
Touchstone/Miramax
Michael Eisner, CEO
500 S. Buena Vista Street
Burbank, CA 91521-1060
(818) 560-4040

Paramount Pictures
Sherry Lansing, CEO
5555 Melrose Avenue

Los Angeles, CA 90038-3197
(213) 956-5000
(213) 956-2007 fax

MGM, Inc. (Metro Goldwyn Mayer)
United Artists/UA
Frank Mancuso, CEO
2500 Broadway Street
Santa Monica, CA 90404-3061
(310) 449-3000

Viacom Inc. (owner of Paramount Pictures)
Sumner M. Redstone, Chairman
1515 Broadway
New York, NY 10036
(212) 258-6000

Orion Pictures Corporation
Leonard White, CEO
1888 Century Park East
Los Angeles, CA 90067
(310) 282-0550

Sony Pictures Entertainment (Columbia/Tri-Star)
Alan Levine, CEO
Culver City, CA 90232
(310) 280-8000

20th Century Fox
Peter Chernin
P.O. Box 900
Beverly Hills, CA 90213
(310) 277-2211

Warner Bros. Studios
Robert Daly, Chairman of the Board
4000 Warner Boulevard
Burbank, CA 91522
(818) 954-6000

(818) 954-3232 fax

News Corporation (owner of 20th Century Fox)
K. Rupert Murdoch, Chairman and CEO
2 Holt Street
Sydney, NSW, Australia 2110

Time Warner, Inc. (owner of Warner Bros. Studios)
Gerald Levin, Chm., President & CEO
1271 Avenue of the Americas
New York, NY 10020
(212) 484-8000

Universal Pictures
Alan Sutton, VP of National Publicity
100 Universal City Plaza
Universal City, CA 91608
(818) 777-1000
(818) 733-1473 fax

You may also want to contact the Motion Picture Association of America, the nonprofit group that provides the rating for all major releases, and the National Association of Theater Owners.
Addresses appear below:

Motion Picture Assn. of America (MPAA)
Jack Valenti
15503 Ventura Boulevard
Encino, CA 90404-3061
(818) 995-3600
(818) 382-1799 fax

National Assn. of Theater Owners
Mary Ann Grasso, Ex. Director
4605 Lankershim Boulevard
North Hollywood, CA 91602
(818) 506-1778
(919) 506-0269 fax

Establish standards for entertainment in your home

I believe it is important that we be discerning about the kind of music we listen to, television programs we watch, and movies that we see. It is also important that every family limit the amount of time they allow for entertainment - even when it's the best films. Too much television usually results in inactivity and boredom. We have become an entertainment-crazed society. Too many of us are sitting around watching when we should be out doing!

It is also important to discern and decide what kinds of objectionable materials we will not allow in our homes: profanity? nudity? sexual scenes? gratification of immorality? the technic promotion of entertainment styles known for their immoral life-styles? The questions are almost endless, but they must be asked, and they must be answered!

Television is just as bad

You may be saying to yourself, "Well, I don't attend movies," but sooner or later the movies find their way on the television and into your living room. They influence the morality of television programs and, in turn, the morality of most Americans. Whether we like it or not, our nation is being inundated by the cesspool unleashed from Hollywood and the other centers of the entertainment world. The LaHayes observe: "What Hollywood sanctions today, the country will probably sanction tomorrow."[9]

Since the average American watches over 7 hours of television a day, we need to take seriously the impact of television on the average American. Even children and teenagers, who spend a good part of their day in school, still watch over 3 hours of television per day. That adds up to over 20 hours of television per week. It is no wonder that pastors and youth ministers, who spend a few hours with Christian teens a week, are limited compared to the impact of more than 20 hours of television broadcasts.

Over the years, television has become an open battlefield in regard to the issue of moral values. There was a time when the immoral life-style of the actors was somewhat hidden from viewers. Then there was a period of subtlety when the character portrayed was a decent human being in every area of his or her life, except in their sexual behavior. Today, there is little difference between the "good guys" and the "bad guys." Most of them lie, steal, cheat, and live sexually immoral lives.

Television has moved to the left so fast that it is barely on the screen anymore, and the irony is that most of the people don't even like what they're viewing! So listing shows that are examples of the kind of immorality that is prevalent on television is almost irrelevant because such shows don't last very long. It is almost as though they offend the viewer to such an extreme that they eventually nullify one's senses and the program eventually loses its sizzle. But it doesn't take a genius to figure out what the basic plots and subplots are all about - sex, sex, and more sex!

The big difference with television in the nineties is there is no distinction between the "good guys" or the "bad guys." The hero or heroine of a sitcom or a dramatic program will generally have as many moral conflicts in their lives as anyone else. For example, in one recent drama aimed at teenagers, the heroine is sleeping with her boyfriend, gets pregnant, gets an abortion and is congratulated by her friends for having the "moral courage" to make such an important decision. Many of the leading characters are portrayed as homosexuals or lesbians, and in the most favorable light possible.

Those who raise moral objections to all of this are often portrayed as fanatics, extremists, and bigots. Even kids' programming, like Dinosaurs, encourage an acceptance of the homosexual life-style. In this particular show, the main couple is a pair of carnivorous meat-eating dinosaur couple. They are surprised to learn that their dinosaur son is a "herbo" who only eats herbs and frequents a "herbo" bar. The emphasis of the program is saying that he is different "by nature" and that we should be open and accepting of his "alternate life-style."[10]

Music from the pits of hell

Any discussion of the impact of the media upon the young people in America is incomplete without an honest look at the staggering impact of the music industry. Teenagers are spending billions of dollars each year for the simple-minded glorification of animal lust! Twenty-four hours a day, MTV promotes a lifestyle that is contrary to any kind of Christian beliefs or values whatever. Songs and lyrics that may be viewed as morally questionable are brought to their complete immoral impact by video imaging. In other words, the pictures make it clear what the words are all about.

The very names of today's rock groups make it obvious what they're all about:

Annihilator	Atrocity
Atheist	Black Sabbath
The Damned	Dark Angel
Demolition	Devastation
Legion of Death	Malice
Massacre	Poison
Slaughter	Social Distortion
Suicidal Tendencies	Denim
Voodoo	Ultimate Revenge

Teenagers try to minimize the dangerous effects of their music and its foul and filthy lyrics by pointing out that it's the beat, and not the words, that are appealing to them, but a recent survey by the University of Florida indicates that 90% of teenagers listening to rock music do know the words, and 60% of them agree with the words. To make things worse, the major themes of rock music are hatred, domestic violence, lust, derision of authority, drugs, violence, and sexual immorality.

The power of these images has captured the minds and hearts of today's young people. They have little chance of withstanding the onslaught of temptation, vulgar language, sex, and drugs when it is being pumped at them day and night over our nation's radio stations.

I am not an expert on music, and I realize there is wide variation in musical tastes, but whenever music is used to promote images that are immoral, degrading, and spiritually destructive - it is wrong! And it is the height of hypocrisy for the media industry, which produces this material and financially benefits from it, to sit back and complain about the drug problems and teenage pregnancies in our nation when it is their music that promotes these things.

I am absolutely shocked that we do not have hundreds of

parents out picketing and demonstrating against these music companies which produce this filth that is aimed at their children. I realize that some of this is due to the fact that some have rejected this type of music and have little or no contact with it, nevertheless in the vast majority of Christian parents there is simply a willful ignorance about their dealing with it. They just plainly don't want to know what they're singing. They don't want to hassle their kids over this issue. They don't want to take the position of a moral and spiritual "gatekeeper" in their own homes, and the tragedy is that the worst kind of child abuse is being pumped into our homes through our own radio and television sets.

What can we do?

The LaHayes offer three basic suggestions for dealing with the problem of the ravaging of the American conscience by Hollywood and the media:[11]

1. Turn it off!

The entire Christian life centers around our spiritual discipline. If we cannot turn off the television sets in our own homes, then we stand little chance of disciplining ourselves to deal with anything else of significance in our lives. It is important that Christian parents know what their kids are watching and control what their kids are watching. When a particular television program consistently violates your Christian standards, don't watch it, and don't let your kids watch it! It is time that we either control our television watching or get rid of our television sets.

2. Make them pay!

Christian boycotting of advertisers who promote unwholesome programming have been successful in the past. Don Wildmon, head of the American Family Association, has targeted advertisers of specific television shows, and urged people to boycott the products that those advertisers are selling. Fortunately, the producers listen to the advertisers, and the advertisers listen to the public.

If there is no public outcry against this kind of programming, we can only expect them to get worse.

3. Teach your children the difference.

Parents need to make it a point to watch television programming with their children so they can discuss the positives and negatives of that which is presented. It is important that we ask crucial and convicting questions: "Do you think the people who wrote this program believe in God? Do they believe in the absolute truth?" This will help the children begin to evaluate the "hidden agenda" of the producers of television programming.

The ultimate blame does not lie with the secular media, but with the Christian community which is caught up and as entranced by the secular media as any other group in America. If we cannot break the bondage of preprogrammed entertainment, we'll be left with no one in this country who can think for themselves. Ask yourself what is every television program, commercial, or movie saying to me personally, and ask yourself what action am I likely to enact as a result of being impacting by this program? We dare not allow ourselves to be deceived by a secular minority who control the media industry and have us believe we are the ones who are out of step with society.

We can make a difference in the area of public entertainment. We cannot stop the personal moral perversions of individuals who are involved with the entertainment industry, however, we can raise a voice of moral objection from our pulpits, our communities, and through our political leaders to object to the infiltration of those antifamily, anti-God, antimoral attitudes they pump into the airwaves of America. The only reason this problem has not been solved sooner is because too many of our pastors and Christian leaders have been afraid to address it. Where are the prophets of today who are willing to stand against the sin of our times? God help us to do it, and do it today!

"Today, America is standing tall. We're rebuilding our defenses setting in place innovative weapons programs and giving you the pay and equipment you need. We're reminding the globe that America still stands for liberty..."

—Ronald Reagan,
Hickam Air Force Base,
April 26, 1986

Chapter 10

National Defense
Fighting For What We Believe

On March 8, 1971, on a battlefield in Vietnam, at 1:30 in the afternoon, I stepped on a land mine. It blew me high in the air. When I came down I was unconscious for a few moments. When I came to there was confusion and commotion all around me. My head hurt as I looked up into the face of a black marine, Corporal Lee Gore. He was a devout Christian and was not ashamed of it. I had seen him read his Bible and I had heard him pray. I knew he lived his testimony in the details of his life.

I had been saved when I was ten years old, and I was raised in a Christian home. As a teenager I became rebellious and tried running from God, but that day I realized I wouldn't be running anywhere, anymore.

As I lay there in the lap of Corporal Gore, I promised God if He would let me live and get back home, I would surrender my life to His will. Before the day was over they had taken me to the hospital ship, the USS Sanctuary. By the second day I was on the ship, two doctors had given up on me, infection set in, and I ran a high temperature. Things were so bad that they didn't expect me to live.

Yet God had other plans for my life. They took me to the Island of Guam where I spent the next two weeks. During that four-week period, my parents received numerous telegrams from the Marine Corps. From a human standpoint, they never expected to see me alive again.

Eventually I began to recover, and they flew me back to the United States to the Philadelphia Naval Hospital. I spent the next 8¹/₂ months there, undergoing 13 major operations and several other surgeries. When it was all over, my legs had been amputated. They left 3 inches on my right leg, and 11 inches on the left leg, although no other part of my body was hurt.

God got my attention on March 8, 1971. I had committed my life to serving America in her military engagement in Southeast Asia, still, on that day, I recommitted my life to Christ and to serving him for all eternity. I say all this to emphasize that my opinions on national defense are not made in a vacuum. These are not the well-intended sentiments of a pastor, sitting in the comforts of his office, who has never faced the seriousness of war. I have been there when we were under the hail of gunfire. I have seen friends and companions shot to death. I have seen others step on land mines and been blown to pieces. I have been there when the bombs were dropping all around us. I know personally the price that some of us had to pay in order for America to remain free.

Nearly 25 years have gone by since that time, and there are some who question our nation's involvement in Vietnam. But I believe God used the commitment of young men and women who were willing to serve Him and their country in that hour of great need. He used us in a time and place when the freedom of the whole world was at stake. Had we not gone to Vietnam and stalled the communist offensive in Southeast Asia, there's no telling how much of the world the communists would have taken. It's not as likely that we would have seen the fall of communism in Eastern Europe in 1989 and in the former Soviet Union in 1991. I'm convinced our efforts in Vietnam stalled the communist offensive and made them eventually give up on the rest of Southeast Asia.

I am also convinced there are times when it is necessary to go to war. Of course, it is not desirable. If there is anyway to have peace with dignity and integrity, then peace is preferred; but when we can only have peace at the price of the surrender of our personal rights and our national integrity, it is a peace that is not worth having! In biblical times, God ordered His people to go to war to defend their beliefs, the sovereignty of their territory, and to protect their families from the tyranny of foreign invasion. So, too, throughout history there have been times when God has obviously intervened in human affairs by the means of war. War is a tragic result of the fall of mankind. The history of war began the day Cain killed his brother, Abel. It is estimated that in the past 5,000 years, men have fought over 14,000 wars. In the last 400 years, modern nations have entered into more than 8,000 peace treaties which have lasted an average of only 2 years each.

During the First World War, 8 1/2 million men and women gave their lives in the war that was supposed to end all wars. In the Second World War, 22 million people were killed, but the two world wars and the conflicts in Korea and Vietnam have been overshadowed by a more serious event. On August 6, 1945, the first atomic weapon was used in war, and the world has never been the same since. The atom bomb was dropped on Hiroshima. A few years later, the first hydrogen bomb was dropped on a small island in the Pacific Ocean in a test bombing, and the island was bombed totally off the map!

A theology of military defense

God is not the author of war. War is the direct result of the depravity of the human heart. Nevertheless, in many cases, war is a necessary response on the part of godly people in order to prevent the tyranny of aggression and to protect the innocent lives of men, women, and children. Many of God's greatest servants were men of war: Moses, Joshua, Gideon, Samson, Saul, and David. They were told to exterminate the Canaanites, the Amalekites, and the enemies of God. King David actually said: "Blessed be the Lord, my strength, which teacheth my hands to war, and my fingers to fight" (Psalm 18:34; 144:1). 1 Chronicles 5:22 states that the people of Israel were delivered in battle because "the war was of God."

In the New Testament five Roman centurions appear in the

biblical record and are presented in a favorable light. One of them, Cornelius (Acts 10), is the first Gentile convert to the Gospel. In Luke 3:14, we read of Roman soldiers coming to John the Baptist to receive the baptism of repentance. While John told them not to deal unjustly with the people, he never rebuked the nature of their occupation as military men.

The Lord Jesus predicted there would be "wars and rumors of wars" throughout the present era. David Jeremiah comments: "Jesus accepts war as a part of the world order and draws from it an impressive illustration of exacting conditions of Christian discipleship."[1] In Romans 13:1-4, the Bible makes it clear that national leaders are viewed as "ministers of God" for the good of the public they serve. They are to execute "wrath" upon evil doers and those who would threaten the lives of others. Therefore, in a fallen and depraved world, it is necessary for national authorities to exist who can maintain law and order within a given society. It is also necessary to protect a sovereign group of people from invasion by hostile forces who would threaten the peace and security of those people. Yes, war is a nasty business, still war is also a necessary business.

The longest era of peace the world may ever have known is the celebrated pax romana, which was made possible by the military might of the Roman Empire. Believe it or not, the best way to avoid war is to have a strong military defense. During the Vietnam War, an American helicopter pilot was killed. His parents had this saying inscribed on his tombstone in New Hampshire. It was taken from the words of John Stuart Miller in the 19th Century.

"War is an ugly thing, but not the ugliest of things. The decayed and degraded state of moral and patriotic feeling, which thinks nothing is worth a war, is worst. A man who has nothing which he cares more about than his own personal safety, is a miserable creature, and has no chance of being free, unless he is made free and kept so by the exertions of better men than himself.[2]

We must face reality

America is a hated nation! Despite the fact that we have invested the lives of some of our finest people, and the efforts of our greatest resources, to help preserve freedom and democracy upon this planet — we are of all nations most unappreciated.

America is the great superpower of the 20th Century. As we enter the 21st Century we have virtually become the leader of the free world. Despite this fact, we are foolish to think we can disarm ourselves and remain free in the future. I am convinced the only reason America won the Cold War is because President Ronald Reagan spent the communists under the table! By revitalizing America's national defenses and being willing to go on the offensive with aggressive revitalization of military forces, President Reagan forced the hand of the communist leaders in the former Soviet Union. They had spent the vast majority of their resources building up a military arsenal with the intention of conquering the world, at the lack of the internal well-being of their own people. Had President Reagan not made the commitment he did, I'm convinced the Cold War would still be going on today.

Let's go back even a further step. Had America's Christian leaders, like Jerry Falwell, James Kennedy, and Tim LaHaye not spoken out against America's military demise under the leadership of President Jimmy Carter, and challenged their people to elect a president who would take a stronger position on these issues, we might still be living with the immediate threat of nuclear war at this very hour. There is no telling what could have happened had God not intervened in this nation's history in the 1980s.

At that time Dr. Falwell wrote:

We must face the fact: America is in serious trouble today; She has economically and militarily lost her prominence among the nations of the world. It is time we as Americans realize that our "peaceful intentions" are acts of stupidity and that the lives of our citizens are at stake.[3]

Today we are at a similar crossroads. Many Americans assume that we can simply disarm ourselves now because the dreaded enemy of communism has been defeated, but I would remind you that while the government has changed hands in

Moscow, and while the Russian flag flies over the nation instead of the Soviet flag — many of the same people are still in power. What is worse, the nuclear weapons that we always feared could be used against us are still there as well! The potential of armed conflict between Russia and the rest of the world is still very much a reality. Look at Russia's ally, Serbia. They are slaughtering the population of the Balkan states. They have no regard for human life. They would just as soon drop a missile on a crowded civilian population as they would on military targets. Most people forget it was Serbian brutality that started World War I, and that Russia came to their defense then and they would again!

America is the most powerful nation in the world for two reasons. Number one, God has ordained it so! This nation has been blessed of God from its very beginning because it was founded on the truths and principles of God's Word. Number two, God has graciously given us the means to defend ourselves. No weapons formed against us have prospered, because God has chosen to defend us. But if we continue to turn our backs on God and the principles of His Word, we cannot continue to expect Him to intervene on our behalf. America is shaking her fist in the face of God and asking Him to send His judgment upon us. What a tragic day that will be when God finally says, "Enough!"

If you want to know what happens to a nation when it turns its back on God - look at the Soviet Union. Marx and Lenin promised to give the world a new future based on a new humanity. But after 70 years of atheism and repression, that humanity was not, as Dr. James Kennedy has noted:

> a noble and selfless paragon of virtue but a monster without a heart and soul. The new man created by the communist nightmare has been systematically deprived of his character and his conscience, along with his nobility, morality, character and ethics. He has been reduced to little more than a wild beast in an urban jungle with no compassion or compunction.[4]

We cannot lower the flag!

I fully realize that America is not synonymous with the kingdom of God. We are not a theocracy. We cannot expect a young regenerate to espouse the same beliefs and values as the people of God. But that does not mean that Christians ought to lower the flag anymore than we ought to drop the banner of Christ.

Our flag is not just another piece of material hanging on a pole. Men and women have given their lives so that flag might fly in freedom over the land of the brave. On June 14, 1777, the Continental Congress stated: "that the flag of thirteen states be 13 stripes, alternate red and white, and that the union be 13 stars, white in a blue field, representing a new constellation."

The designers of our flag gave the definition of the symbolism of its colors. White, they said, would signify the purity and innocence of our nation. Red would represent the heartiness and valor of our people. Blue would signify vigilance, perseverance and justice.

That flag was birthed in the blood of the American Revolution. It represents more than governmental politics. It represents everything this nation was founded for in the first place. Notice again the characteristics symbolized by the flag: purity, innocence, heartiness, valor, vigilance, perseverance, and justice. When these qualities cease to exist in the hearts and souls of Americans, the meaning and purpose for which this nation was established will have vanished. The flag may continue to fly for a while, but it will be an empty symbol of a nation that has committed moral and spiritual suicide.

Think of the people who have died for what that flag represents. Before the Battle of Bennington in Vermont, General John Starke rounded up some militiamen from Vermont and New Hampshire to fight the British. He cried, "Tonight the American flag floats from yonder hill or Molly Starke sleeps a widow!" Before the day was over, the Americans had won a tremendous victory over the British forces.

That same flag was flown above the troops at Saratoga in New York, and over the nearly frozen bodies of our men at Valley Forge, Pennsylvania. That flag flew above the head of Mary Hayes, a brave woman who assisted her husband in firing his cannon during the Battle of Monmouth in New Jersey. That same flag flew at Yorktown when the British commander, Cornwallis, surrendered to General George Washington.

The American flag was posted in Constitution Hall in Philadelphia, and it was posted during the rolling drum salute and the firing of the muskets in the military ceremony when it replaced the French tricolor in the City of New Orleans on December 20, 1803, as the Louisiana Territory was transferred from France to the United States.

Yet today, people trample underfoot the flag that men have given their lives for in two world wars. That flag was not meant for burning but for waving. If you're ashamed to stand by your colors, you need to serve another flag. These colors don't run! God pity the nation who forgets the blood of its own people who have suffered to keep it free!

I gave my two legs, and nearly gave my life for what that flag represents, and I have absolutely no patience with those who would belittle its significance, decry its stature, or deny the freedoms that it represents. What hypocrisy! The very people who have been the worst critics of this nation and its military have enjoyed a freedom of speech to denounce the very freedoms that the blood of real American patriots paid for. God help us! Such people ought to be denounced as traitors! If they really hate this country so much, let them leave and go find another one that is better!

I have traveled all over the world, and there is no other nation like America! There is not a nation that has the kind of religious freedom and economic security that Americans have enjoyed. There is no nation who cares about the suffering of others around the world like America has. We did not have to get involved with World War I, World War II, or Vietnam, or the Persian Gulf. We could have just sat back and let the world go to hell. But that's not the American way! A nation founded by God-fearing Bible-believing people cannot sit back and permit injustice and tyranny to rule the world. We who have been set free by the power of the gospel understand what true freedom is really all about, and when the cause of freedom is at stake, we must stand up and defend it at all costs!

Our ultimate defense is God

While military prowess is necessary in order to defend one's self against tyranny and aggression, the greatest defense of all is the power of God. Without His blessing, no nation can stand, no matter how many weapons it possesses, or how large an army it fields. The scripture reminds us: "If God be for us, who can be against us?" (Romans 8:31).

Two hundred years ago, Professor Alexander Tyler wrote the following words about the fall of the great civilizations of the past. He said: "The average age of the world's great civilizations has been 200 years. These nations have progressed through the following sequence: From bondage to spiritual faith, from spiritual faith to great courage, from courage to liberty, from liberty to abundance, from abundance to selfishness, from selfishness to complacency, from complacency to apathy, from apathy to dependency, and from dependency back to bondage."[5]

If Tyler is correct, America is living on borrowed time. We are already in the complacency and apathy stages and moving rapidly toward dependency. Some believe we may have already gone beyond the point of no return.

In 1835, Alexis de Tocqueville visited America from France, searching for the secret to our nation's greatness. At that time, the Frenchman wrote: "I sought for the greatness and genius of America and her commodious harbor and ample rivers and it was not there. Not until I went into the churches of America and heard her pulpits aflame with righteousness did I understand the secret of her power. America is great because she is good. If America ever ceases to be good, she will cease to be great."[6]

The bottom line is still the same — America must be good if she is to be great, and America must remain strong if she is to remain free. In the grace of God, He has allowed this nation of ours to rise to such greatness, not because we deserve it in and of ourselves, but because we have preserved the freedom of religion and the propagation of the gospel - not only in our nation but from those shores it has reached around the world.

God does not need America: America needs God! We cannot hope to remain free and turn our backs on the source of freedom itself. We cannot hope to do anything powerful and turn away from the true source of our power. The Bible continues to shout down through the halls of history and the corridor of time: "Blessed is that nation whose God is the Lord."

"Revival is not an option.
It is a necessity! We can't just
hope for a spiritual awakening.
We must have one!"

—Tim Lee
Evangelist

Chapter 11

National Revival
America's Greatest Need

There are many great issues facing America today, but there is no issue greater than the need for national spiritual revival. Psalm 85:6 says, "Wilt thou not revive us again: that thy people may rejoice in thee?" These are two things that always go together, according to this text: revival and rejoicing. You cannot have the one without the other. If there is a genuine, holy ghost-empowered revival, it will result in true and lasting joy, and where there is rejoicing among the people of God because their hearts are right with God, there will always come a spirit of true and genuine revival.

Dr. Edward Hindson, Professor of Religion at Liberty University in Virginia, has observed:

> Genuine revival has always been the method through which the outpouring of the spirit of God has come upon the church. Through the ages of church history, time and time again, God has moved to bless His church in a very wonderful way.[1]

135

As I have traveled across this nation every week since 1979, I must confess that there is little evidence of genuine revival in America today. There is definitely a hunger for God. There is a longing for "times of refreshing" to come from the Lord. There is a general acknowledgment that we need revival, but there still is no national revival on the horizon at this moment.

We have all read the reports of the initial stirrings of God on campuses of some of our state universities and some of our major Christian colleges. Hundreds of students are beginning to pray and seek the face of God. Many are publicly confessing their sins and their indifference to the things of God. It is as though the young people of our nation are realizing the emptiness of a culture without God. They seem to sense that once you turn your back on God, you are left with nothing of any real significance and value.

But that kind of revival has yet to shake our churches, communities, and public institutions in this land. Socially, politically, and religiously, things look bleak in America, but let me remind you that sometimes you have to get to the bottom of the barrel before you're willing to look up.

We may be living in the best time in America to see a great spiritual awakening. I believe there is still hope for America and hope for the future.

Our politicians tell us we need better laws. Our educators tell us we need more funds for the educational systems of our nation. Sociologists tell us we need to restructure our basic social units. Psychologists tell us we need a greater sense of inner stability and meaning and purpose in our lives. But all of these pale into insignificance in light of our greatest need; and that is for a God-sent spiritual awakening that would sweep this nation like a prairie fire. We need revival in our homes, our churches, our schools, in our cities, and in our nation — at every level.

A spiritual revival

The nation of Israel was indeed blessed of God. They had been called by Him out of bondage in Egypt. He had sustained them in the wilderness and went before them in the conquest of the Promised Land. But over the years, the people of God began to turn away from the things of God, and, in time, they began to turn away from God Himself. In their darkest hour, the Prophet Jeremiah came to the people of Israel, and told them that they needed a spiritual revival.

Jeremiah said:

> "Hath a nation changed their gods, which are yet no gods; but my people have changed their glory for that which doeth not profit. Be astonished O ye heavens at this and be horribly afraid, be ye very desolate saith the Lord. For my people have committed two evils; they have forsaken the fountain of living waters and hewed them out cisterns, broken cisterns that can hold no water" (Jeremiah 2:11-13).

Notice that the people of God had surrendered their glory (meaning crown) for the things of the world. They had surrendered the glory of God for the wisdom of the world. They had exchanged the beauty of holiness for the pleasure of fleshly carnality, and in all of this, they had forgotten God.

Knowing God is our glory! Serving God is our greatest joy, and when revival comes, God's people are drawn into a more intimate relationship with Him than ever before. On that basis, I believe I can say there is no glory in our churches today. The glory has departed and we have been left with the empty rituals and traditions of religion without the presence and power of God, not only in liberal churches, but in many of our fundamental and evangelical churches as well.

The anointing of God has departed from our churches, our Christian schools, and our Christian colleges and seminaries. Walk in the average church today and watch the people. There is no fire - no zeal. Why? Because there is no sense of the presence of God!

We must remember that revival begins with God's people. 2 Chronicles 7:14 says:

> If my people, which are called by my name, shall humble themselves, and pray, and seek my faceturn from their wicked ways; then will I hear from heaven, and will forgive their sin, and heal their land.

Whenever I preach out against the liberals, the flag burners, and the moral perverts in our nation, people get stirred up, and well they should! But God has burdened my heart to realize the greatest need for revival is among our own churches and among our own people!

It is one thing to preach against the sins of others, but when we begin to deal with the sin in our lives, then, and only then, will God be glorified. Then and only then, will God begin to work in our lives. Then we will see a spiritual awakening among those who claim the name of God, and when that happens, there will be hope for a spiritual awakening among the unbelieving public as well.

Until we realize that sin and wickedness abound in the house of God, and that is the ultimate source of the problems in our nation, we will never experience revival.

The Apostle Paul said of Israel, "For if God spared not the natural branches, take heed lest he also spare not thee" (Romans 11:21). God doesn't owe America anything! God will bring judgment on this nation just as He has brought judgment on every other nation that has rejected him!

In the Book of Lamentations, (3:40), the Prophet Jeremiah challenged the people of God when he said, "Let us search and try our ways, and turn again to the Lord." That's repentance! Then the Prophet went on to say, "Let us lift our hands unto God in the heavens." That's praise and worship! When we repent of our sins and praise and worship the Lord in a spirit of brokenness and humility, the glory of God will return unto our midst.

Patriotic revival

During the 1960's and the 1970's, patriotism in America was at an all-time low. Some had already lost hope that it could ever be revived, but as we approached the Bicentennial in 1976 there was a sudden revival of patriotism in our nation. The 200th anniversary of the signing of the Declaration of Independence seemed to recapture our national conscience. People began to realize afresh what this nation and its freedoms were really all about, and for the next several years, patriotism began to soar again in America. During the twelve years of the presidential administrations of Ronald Reagan and George Bush, patriotism continued to soar, reaching an apex during the Gulf War in 1989-90.

But since then, patriotism has been in a steady and dramatic decline. Young people have become disillusioned with the corruption of politics which has been constantly exposed to the press during the presidency of Bill Clinton. Many have lost confidence in the very nature and character of the office of the presidency because of Bill and Hillary Clinton's constant acceptance and promotion of immoral life-styles. Our First Couple have surrounded themselves with people of questionable moral values and personal integrity, and sadly, patriotism has begun to decline.

This condition should not surprise us. When he was running for president, Bill Clinton openly acknowledged that he had avoided the draft during the Vietnam War because he was unwilling to serve his country in its hour of need. What do you think that says to a Vietnam veteran like myself? "It's okay for you to go to Vietnam and lose your legs for our national freedoms, but I'm too important to give anything of myself in that measure of sacrifice."

Do you think that I, or anyone like me, has one ounce of respect for that kind of attitude? Not on your life! Bill Clinton is a coward, and needs to be thrown out of office! On July 8, 1991, I spoke at a special Patriotic Rally at the First Baptist Church, Springdale, Arkansas. There were approximately 2,500 in attendance, including then Governor of Arkansas, Bill Clinton. During the invitation to receive Christ as Savior, approximately 25 people raised their hand to indicate they were personally giving their lives to Christ that night. Among them was Bill Clinton. Photos of the Governor, with an upraised hand, appeared in our magazine, *Target*, (October 1992), and when candidate Clinton was questioned about the nature of his "conversion" on that night, denied that he was making that commitment at that time.

I realize that President Clinton claims to be a born-again Christian, that he attends the Emmanuel Baptist Church in Little Rock, Arkansas, and that he even carries a Bible with him to church. All of these things are commendable, but none of these things will transform his life.

The Bible tells us we can only judge a tree by its fruit, and the fruit of President Clinton's Administration in the White House has been abominable, to say the least. He has openly courted homosexuals, lesbians, feminists, and ungodly entertainers. He has appointed some of the worst-possible people to positions of leadership in his administration. Do I even need to comment on Janet Reno, or Jocelyn Elders; I cannot judge the heart of any human being. Only God can do that!

But the outward indication of all the evidence we have seen for the past three years would lead us to believe that President and Mrs. Clinton are anything but true believers. They certainly are not the epitome of the kind of positive Christianity that will turn this nation back to God, and as long as they remain in the leadership of this nation, we cannot expect God to bless us. President Clinton has openly advocated his support of abortion, homosexuality, and situation ethics. Every time moral, spiritual and ethical questions have been raised in regard to President Clinton's leadership, he has done everything in his power to sweep the issue under the rug. This is not the kind of leadership we need; this is not the kind of patriotism we need; and God help us if we have to endure four more years of it!

Patriotism alone will not save America. We must not confuse a revival of patriotism with a revival of spirituality. They are not the same thing, but they often go hand in hand. You cannot love God and hate that which He has blessed. You cannot know God and fail to see the handwork of God in our nation's history. But unless we experience a genuine revival, His hand of blessing will be removed, and it will return against us as the hand of judgment!

Revival: the real thing

Genuine revival is the result of the work of God in the hearts of men. Whatever God produces will bear the stamp of His approval. Consider that real revival will always involve these basic characteristics:

1. Revival comes when people pray.

Every great revival in the history of the church has come as the result of the impassioned prayers of men and women of God. William McColloch, the pastor at Cambuslang, Scotland, prayed continually day and night for revival for over a year before God burst upon his congregation in February, 1742. Evan Roberts prayed for a revival daily for 13 years before the famous Welch Revival of 1904 became a reality. Within 5 months, over 100,000 people were converted to Christ as a result of his praying. Dr. Horatius Bonar has said of those great men of the past:

> They were much alone with God, replenishing their own souls out of the living fountain that out of them might flow to their people rivers of living water.[2]

The Prophet Hosea preached a revival message to the nation of Israel during its darkest hour. He pled with the people and said, "Sow to yourselves righteousness, reap in mercy, break up your fallow ground." Fallow ground is unplowed ground. For many Christians their "fallow ground" is their prayer life.

The time has come for us to break up our fallow ground by seeking the Lord in prayer. Until we get on our faces before God and continually cry out to God for revival, there will be no revival.

Can a nation be changed by the prayers of just a few? Yes! John Knox prayed: "Give me Scotland, else I die!" Evan Roberts prayed for Wales and got it! John Wesley prayed for England in her time of desperate spiritual need and prevailed!

2. Revival comes by the declaration of the Word of God.

Our greatest problem in America is not that we're not being preached to! There is plenty of preaching going on but little of it is directed toward the real problems in our nation. Truth is truth! When a person who is interested in the truth hears the truth, it will move him to think about himself, his nation, and his God.

We need the kind of preaching today that will stir the hearts and souls of our people. We need the type of preaching that will convict the sinner, correct the backslider, and challenge the believer. We need the kind of preaching that is not afraid to declare, "thus sayeth the Lord." We need the kind of preaching that upholds righteousness, condemns unrighteousness, and calls this nation back to God.

I'm convinced one of the greatest reasons why there is so little fear of God in our society today is that our preachers have failed to preach in the power of the Spirit of God from the truths of the Word of God.

Too many of our religious leaders lack the spiritual power to move the hearts of men and women toward the things of God. Therefore, they are content to substitute a mass of gimmicks, techniques, and methods designed to psychologically affect the passions of people.

When this happens, genuine repentance, faith and holiness go out the window! Without the proclamation of the truths of the Word of God there can be no genuine work of the Spirit of God.

3. Revival comes with the conviction of sin.

Genuine conviction, confession, and repentance are the results of the work of the Holy Spirit. The Bible reminds us: "For godly sorrow worketh repentance to salvation" (2 Cor. 7:10). Although the preaching of repentance has always held a prominent place in the scriptures, it has been neglected in the twentieth century. Therefore, we should not be surprised that ours is one of the most carnal and unspiritual generation of believers ever to name the name of Christ. This neglect is the major reason why believers, as well as unbelievers, have virtually no conviction about the reality of sin.

Whenever there is genuine revival, and the standards of the word of God confront the sinner with the reality of the sin and the severity of God's anger against that sin, the result will be a genuine conviction of sin, conversion of soul, and transformation of life.

The entertainment-oriented evangelism of the twentieth century has fallen short at this very point. There is no revival because there is no conviction of sin. In some cases we have so overemphasized the grace of God that we have neglected the law of God.

We have been so quick to call the sinners to conversion that we have forgotten to call them to repentance; and without repentance there will be no true and lasting salvation.

4. Revival results in substantial and abiding fruit.

The proclamation of the gospel must be accompanied by the sincere and genuine lives of godly people. The reality of our lives enforces the testimony of our message. They are living examples of God's truth, and it is this kind of testimony that the world so desperately needs to see today. In an age when young people have become so bitter and cynical about the realities of life, they must see the reality of Christ is in our lives!

The Apostle Paul explained this very thing to the Corinthian Church when he told them that if an unbeliever came into their midst and was "convinced of all" he would fall on his face and "worship God, and report that God is in you of a truth" (1 Cor. 14:24-25).

This passage makes it clear that God uses fruit-bearing Christians to produce conviction in the unbeliever by the power of the Holy Spirit. Too many of our "converts" return to the world and to careless and ungodly living. They give little or no evidence of any transformation of the Holy Spirit in their lives, but if genuine revival comes from the Spirit of God, it will transform the lives of the people of God. Those who confess to be converted will lead lives that are exemplary of the transforming grace and power of God.

In his classic *Lectures on Revival*, W.B. Sprague said that such life-changing revival is the result of "the more copious and sudden effusion of the Holy Spirit."[3] It was this kind of revival that Sprague, a nineteenth century theologian, called the "final and complete triumph of the church." Oh, that God would bring such triumph today! Oh, that He might rend the heavens and pour out His power as never before on our spiritually desperate land. Revival is not an option — it is the only option! Revival is not one hope among many — it is the only hope for America and the future!

What can one man do?

One man transformed the face of human history — Jesus Christ, the Son of God. He alone made it possible for us to be liberated from the bondage of human sin and misery. He alone made it possible for men and women to be set free by the power of God Almighty. His one life, lived on this earth for 33 years, made all the difference for time and eternity!

One man, the Apostle Paul, transformed by the living Savior, in turn, was used of God to transform the world of the first century. That one man tramped across mountain ranges, swamp infested plains, and risked his life time and time again to proclaim the good news that Jesus Christ had died for our sins, risen from the dead, and is alive for evermore. The whole landscape of the Mediterranean World is dotted with churches and converts who came to the Savior because of the impact of that one man.

In the early Middle Ages, one man - Patrick - a missionary, went to Ireland and risked his life for the cause of Christ; withstanding the elements and the attacks of demon-inspired Druid priests, and was used of God to single-handedly convert the people of Ireland to Christ.

In 1645, Oliver Cromwell gained control of the English Parliament by one vote. As a result, he led the Puritan Reformation of England, and brought about a revival of biblical righteousness among the English people.

In his incredible book, *The Changing of the Guard*, George Grant reminds us that "...in 1776 one vote determined that English, not German, would be the official American language. In 1845 one vote brought Texas into the Union. In 1860, one vote determined that the radical Unitarians would gain control of the Republican Party, sparking the war between the states. In 1923 one vote gave Adolph Hitler control of the Nazi Party and eventually led to World War II. In 1960, John F. Kennedy defeated Richard Nixon by less that one vote per precinct, and the drubbing the Democrats received in the midterm election in 1994 averaged out to less than one vote lost per precinct nationwide."[4]

Need I say any more? It is obvious that God and God alone can move upon this nation whenever, wherever, however He chooses; but the history of the Christian Church tells us without a doubt, that when God moves, He always moves through His people, and God is moving today to stir the hearts and souls of Christian Americans to call for the kind of national revival and spiritual awakening that will bring this nation to repentance, to its knees in prayer, and to a transformation of heart that will result in a revival of holy living.

When Newt Gingrich gives the closing remarks in the *Republicans' Contract with America*, he writes:

> When you hear gunshots in your nation's capital at night, and you know that young Americans have died needlessly, then I would suggest to you that we have every reason to have the moral courage to confront every weakness of the current structure and to replace it.[5]

If Newt Gingrich can say that about America's need for political revival and renewal, then certainly we can say it about America's need for spiritual revival and renewal. God help us to have the courage to stand up for our convictions, and demand that this nation be returned to moral sanity and to its spiritual heritage! God give us the grace to enact a Christian Contract with America that will result in the transformation of this nation by the power of Almighty God, and if it happens, our children and grandchildren will stand up and call us blessed!

I pray that God will continue to
provide the courage, to decision
making men and women, to stand
with me for God and country...
for is there not a cause?

—Tim Lee
Evangelist

Chapter 12

Spiritual Awakening
A Necessity

Since 1979, I have crisscrossed this great nation preaching a message entitled, "America, the Crown Has Fallen." This message is based on Lamentations 5:16, "The crown is fallen from our head: woe unto us, that we have sinned!"

Almost immediately people began to wake up - pastors, politicians, educators, and people in our nation's military. Truth is truth, and when people of character hear the truth, they will always be moved to action.

One of the great truths of this century is the fact that God ordained this United States of America to preserve freedom on earth and to perpetuate the gospel of Jesus Christ around the world.

America's freedom has been defended on the field of battle by our great and noble armies - from the revolution to the Gulf War, but that alone is not why we are free. We are a free people because our freedom has been protected and preserved by God. Bullets alone could not protect this nation: it is obedience to the Book of God that has guaranteed our freedom.

We live in a nation founded by God-fearing people who

came to these shores to worship the true and living God. Why did they risk their lives to come here in the first place? They crossed the ocean in God's name, sent by Him to raise the standard of His Kingdom in the New World. They came as a voice in the wilderness, crying: "Prepare ye the way of the Lord, make his paths straight."

This nation was not built by God-hating, Christ-denying liberals, humanists and secularists, and if they ever gain full control over this nation it won't last one generation! Not one time did our forefathers seek to exclude God from this great nation. In fact, they included Him in everything they did. They prayed, they read and quoted scripture, and they incorporated the moral laws of God into the legal statutes of our society.

Two hundred years ago people took God seriously. They really believed He existed, that He was sovereign over the affairs of men, and that He could indeed bless this nation if we honored Him. When the pilgrims arrived here in 1620, they brought their families, their furniture, their farm implements - but most of all, they brought the Bible! They came seeking the freedom to worship God.

Today, men and women of faith are ridiculed in the media, disclaimed in the press and shunned by the "politically correct" (actually, the spiritually incorrect)! We are labeled bigots, fanatics and extremists because we love God, His word, and His Church. Our spiritual devotion is even labeled by some misguided psychologists as psychologically "unhealthy."

Imagine! A sin-sick society calling godly people unhealthy. I'll tell you what is unhealthy - a sexually permissive society, homosexual perversion, secular atheism, unholy pornography, and the slaughter of millions of innocent children by the means of abortion. That's unhealthy! It's unhealthy for the unborn. It's unhealthy for traditional values. It's unhealthy for the Christian home and family. It's unhealthy for God-fearing people, and it's unhealthy for America!

We need to repent of our sins as a nation. We need to get on our knees and acknowledge our greed, our selfishness, our materialism, our immorality and our tolerance of evil and perversion in this society. We need to ask God to forgive our sins, to change our hearts, and to heal our land.

If we are going to see America saved and safe for future generations, we must stand up and speak up now, before it is too late. This is no time for hesitation. It is a time for action. We must take back the soul of America now. We must let the unbelieving world know enough is enough! We will not sit back and be silent any longer. If it costs us our time and effort - so be it! If it costs us security and convenience - so be it! If it costs us our lives - so be it!

Revival is not an option. It is a necessity! We can't just hope for a spiritual awakening. We must have one! Will you begin to pray with us for that kind of awakening in America? Will you pray for that kind of awakening in your own heart?

The Marines claim they are looking for a "few good men." I believe God is looking for many! He is looking for Christian men and women who will dedicate their time, talents and treasure to do everything they can to call America back to God: to speak up on public issues; to write letters of protest when necessary; to boycott sponsors of ungodly filth; to go to the polls and vote our convictions, and to do all we can to give America one more chance to turn back to God.

To contact Dr. Tim Lee, please write:

Tim Lee Ministries
P.O. Box 461674
Garland, TX 75046

Endnotes

Preface

1. Tim Lee, "A Spiritual Contract with America," *Target,* Vol. 10, No. 2 (Feb. 1995), pp.1-9; 17.

Chapter One

1. *Contract with America,* ed. Ed Gillespie and Bob Schellhas (New York: Times Books for the Republican National Committee, 1994).
2. Ibid, p.4
3. Ibid, p. 7.
4. Cal Thomas, *"Do We Have Any King but Caesar?"* National Liberty Journal (May 1995), p. 20.
5. George Grant, *The Changing of the Guard* (Nashville: Broadman & Holman, 1995), p. 2.
6. William Bennett, *The Index of Leading Cultural Indicators* (Washington, D.C.: Heritage Foundation, 1993), p. 1.
7. Robert Hutchins, *The Conflict in Education in a Democratic Society* (Westport, CT: Greenwood Press, 1973).
8. Francis Schaeffer, *"Dancing Alone,"* quoted in Tim Lee, *"A Spiritual Contract with America,"* Target, Vol. 10, No. 2 (1995), p. 6.
9. George Grant, op. cit, p.p. 13-14.
10. Jerry Falwell, *Listen America!* (Garden City, NY: Doubleday, 1980), p. 21.

Chapter Two

1. Thomas Elliff, *American on the Edge* (Oklahoma City: MCM Press, 1992 (p. 44).
2. Ibid, p. 45.
3. Joseph Scheidler, *"Interview,"* in Target, Vol. 6, No. 1 (January 1991), p. 5.
4. Norman Giesler, quoted in *Target* (January, 1991), p. 7.
5. Laird Harris, ed. *Theological Wordbook of the Old Testament,* (Chicago: Moody Press, 1980), Vol. 2, p. 690.
6. Ibid., Vol 1 , p. 165.
7. Taken from *"Abortion Clinics-An Inside Look,"* Reprinted in Target, vol. 10; No. 1 (January 1995), pp. 12, 17-18.
8. Jerry Falwell, *If I Should Die Before I Wake* (Nashville:

Thomas Nelson, 1986), reprinted in Target, Vol. 5 No. 1 (January 1990), p. 6.

Chapter Three

1. Jerry Falwell, *The New American Family,* (Dallas: Word Publishing, 1992), p. 91.
2. Ibid. p. 94.
3. Tom Elliff, *America on the Edge* (Oklahoma City: MCN Press, 1992), p. 19.
4. National Liberty Journal, Vol. 24, No. 406 (May 1995), p.5.
5. James Dobson, *"Family Issues Alert,"* quoted in the National Liberty Journal, ibid. p. 5.
6. James Dobson, quoted in Moral Majority Report, (July 30, 1980), p. 11.
7. Quoted in Moral Majority Report (March 14, 1980), p. 5.
8. R. Quededeaux, *The Worldly Evangelicals* (New York: Harper and Row, 1978), p. 126.
9. Newsweek (July 20, 1992), p. 55.
10. Op. cit. p. 20.
11. Michael Medved, quoted in information from Focus on the Family, p.1.
12. Josh McDowell, *Right from Wrong* (Dallas: Word Publishing, 1994).
13. Rowland Methaway, *Missing Core Values,* (Cox News Service) Nov. 3, 1993.
14. Ibid., p. 10.
15. William Bennett, quoted in the Pastor's Weekly Briefing from Focus on the Family, Vol. 3, No. 21 (May 26, 1995), p.1.

Chapter Four

1. Jay Strack, *Drugs and Drinking* (Nashville: Thomas Nelson, 1985) pp. 2-25.
2. *"Twelve Things You Should Know about Marijuana,"* Consumers Research (April 1990) pp. 1-2.
3. Strack, op. cit., p. 27.
4. Quoted in Jay Strack, *Good Kids Who Do Bad Things,* (Dallas: Word Publishers, 1993), p. 164.
5. Strack, Drugs and Drinking, p. 59.
6. Ibid. p. 66.

Chapter Five

1. *A Contract with America* (New York Times Books, 1994), p. 42.
2. Contract with America, pp. 37-57.
3. Tim LaHaye *Faith of our Founding Fathers* (Brentwood, TN: Wolgemuth & Hyatt, 1987) p. 9.
4. Ed Dobson and Ed Hindson, *The Seduction of Power* (Old Tappan, NJ: Fleming Revell, 1988), p. 66.
5. R.C. Sproul, Life Views: *Understanding the Ideas that Shape Society Today* (Old Tappan, NY: Fleming Revell, 1986), p. 207.
6. Op. cit. pp. 66-67.

Chapter Six

1. Greg Bahnsen, *Homosexuality: A Biblical View* (Grand Rapids: Baker Book House, 1978), p. 28.
2. Ibid. p.48-59.
3. Quoted in Target, Vol. 10, Number 2 (April 1995), p. 9.
4. Jerry Falwell,*Listen America!*(Garden City, NY: Doubleday, 1980), p. 181.
5. Judith Waldrop, *"You'll Know It's the 21st Century When..."* American Demographics, (Dec. 1990) p. 22.
6. Stanton Jones, *"Homosexuality According to Science,"* (Christianity Today, August 18, 1989,) pp. 26-29.
7. Christine Gorman, *"Invincible AIDS,"* USA Today, August 3, 1992), p. 34.
8. Department of Health and Human Services, Public HealthService, Centers for Disease Control, Center for Prevention Services, 1991, Division of STD/HIV, Prevention Annual Report, p. 13.
9. David Jeremiah, *Before It's Too Late* (Nashville:1981) pp. 35-37.

Chapter Seven

1. Judith Wallerstein and S. Blakeslee, *Second Chances: Men, Women, and Children —After Divorce* (New York: Pickner, Pickering and Fields, 1989) p. 84ff.
2. Myron Magnet, *"The American Family,* 1992, Fortune, August 10, 1992), p. 42.
3. Jerry Falwell, *The New American Family* (Dallas: Word Publishing, 1992), p. 1.

4. Op. cit., p. 83.
5. Joe Klein, *"Whose Values,"* Newsweek (June 8, 1992), p. 19-22.
6. Op. cit., p. 31.
7. James Dobson and Gary Bauer, *Children at Risk,* Dallas: Word Publishing, 1990), pp. 110-113.
8. Edith Schaeffer, *What Is a Family?,* (Old Tappan, NJ: Simon Revell, 1979), p. 69.
9. Excerpts from a speech delivered by Vice President Dan Quayle to the Commonwealth Club in San Francisco, CA, May 20, 1992.
10. Randall Terry, *Accessory to Murder: The Enemies and Allies and Accomplices to the Death of Our Culture* (Broadhead, TN: Worgemuth and Hyatt, 1990), p. 15.
11. Rebecca Havelin, *Banning Prayer Is Wrong,* USA Today (June 25, 1992).
12. Jerry Falwell, The New American Family, p. 112.

Chapter Eight

1. Jesse Helms, *"Forward",* in Everett Koop, *The Right to Live: the Right to Die* (Wheaton, IL, Tyndale House, 1976), p. 12.
2. Ibid., p. 17.
3. Joseph Fletcher, Situation Ethics: the New Morality (Philadelphia: Westminster, 1966), p. 123.
4. David Jeremiah, *If It's Too Late* (Nashville: Thomas Nelson, 1982), p. 79.
5. Carl Henry, *"Love without Law,"* Christianity Today (October 8, 1965), p. 33.
6. Op. cit. p. 85.
7. Norman Anderson, *Issues of Life and Death,* (Downers Grove, IL: Intervarsity Press, 1977), pp. 34-35.
8. Ibid. pp. 36-37.
9. Joni Eareckson Tada, *When Is It Right to Die* (San Francisco: Harper, San Francisco, 1992), pp. 19-20.
10. Ibid. p. 58.

Chapter Nine

1. Michael Medved, *Hollywood vs. America,* (New York: Harper Collins, 1992), p. 3.
2. Ibid. p. 5.
3. Tim and Beverly LaHaye, *A Nation without A Conscience,*

(Wheaton, IL: Tyndale House, 1994), pp.197-198.
4. Quoted in Medved, op. cit., pp. 344-345.
5. TV: The World's Greatest Bind-bender, (New York: Morality in Media, 1993), p. 7-8.
6. Tom Elliff, *America on the Edge,* (Oklahoma City, MCM Press, 1992), pp. 11-12.
7. Ted Baehr, *"Miracle on Main Street?"* Focus on the Family (Apr. 1995), p. 3.
8. Ted Baehr, *"Miracle on Main Street?"* Focus on the Family (Apr. 1995), p. 3.
9. Ibid.
10. Tim and Beverly LaHaye, op. cit., pp. 209-210.
11. *"Childhood,"* published by Family Research Council, p. 70, quoted by Elliff, op. cit.,   p. 13.
12. Op. cit., pp. 213-215.

Chapter Ten
1. David Jeremiah, *Before It's Too Late* (Nashville, Thomas Nelson, 1982). p. 145.
2. Quoted in David Jeremiah, *Before It's Too Late*, p. 149.
3. Jerry Falwell, *Listen America!,* (Garden City, NY: Doubleday, 1980), p. 97.
4. D. James Kennedy, *Character & Destiny*, (Grand Rapids: Zondervan, 1994), p. 130.
5. Alexander Tyler, quoted by David Jeremiah, op. cit. p. 167.
6. Alexis de Tocqueville, *Democracy in America,* Vol. 1,(New York, Vintage Books, 1945 Edition) p. 319

Chapter Eleven
1. Edward E. Hindson, *Glory in the Church* (Nashville: Thomas Nelson 1975) p. 26.
2. Ibid. p. 64.
3. W.B. Sprague, Lectures on Revival (Edenburgh: Banner of Truth, 1978 reprint of 1832 Edition), p. 3.
4. George Grant, *The Changing of the Guard* (Nashville: Broadman & Holman, 1995), pp. 185-186.
5. *Contract with America* (New York: Titus Books, 1994), p. 195.